Building
STRUCTURES
for Your Garden Railway

Jack Verducci

Published by
Kalmbach Books
21027 Crossroads Circle
Waukesha, Wisconsin 53186
www.Kalmbach.com/Books

© 2010 Jack Verducci. All rights reserved. This book may not be reproduced in part or in whole without the written permission of the publisher, except in the case of brief excerpts for review.

Published in 2010

14 13 12 11 10   1 2 3 4 5

Manufactured in the United States of America

ISBN: 978-0-89024-719-8

The material in this book has previously appeared as articles in *Garden Railways* magazine.

Publisher's Cataloging-In-Publication Data

Verducci, Jack.
   Building structures for your garden railway / by Jack Verducci.

      p. : ill. ; cm. -- (Garden railways books)

   "The material in this book has previously appeared as articles in Garden railways magazine."
      ISBN: 978-0-89024-719-8

1. Railroads--Models. 2. Railroads--Models--Design and construction. I. Title. II. Title: Garden railways.

TF197 .V472 2010
625.1/9

Contents

Introduction 4

Chapter 1 Plastic cement, glues, and adhesives 6

Chapter 2 Tools 13

Chapter 3 Kits 21

Chapter 4 Scratchbuilding 26

Chapter 5 Basic wood construction 31

Chapter 6 Advanced wood construction 37

Chapter 7 Doors, windows, and trim 46

Chapter 8 Plastic fabrication 51

Chapter 9 Building with Styrofoam and Precision Board 60

Chapter 10 Magic Sculp epoxy putty 66

Chapter 11 Casting resin parts for your buildings 69

Chapter 12 Textured walls and roofs 77

Chapter 13 Painting for protection and finish 84

Chapter 14 Landscaping with model structures 90

Chapter 15 Lighting 96

Gallery Detailing the Crystal Club Bar 102

Animating a steam-operated sawmill 105

Detailing Brown's Machine Shop 109

In this 1993 photo of my railroad, there are several types of real-life construction methods modeled, including board-and-batten, planked, novelty siding, and clapboard. Several methods of model construction are also represented—plank-on-solid, hardboard shell, cast resin, plywood shell, and styrene.

Introduction

It could be argued that structures are one of the most important features of a garden railroad. Structures give a railroad purpose and make it come alive. Structures can also set the mood, location, and time period of the railroad. Even if you run trains frequently, you still look at the buildings more often than the trains. After all, a train doesn't run continuously, but the buildings are always in sight.

There are many ways to approach a building project. In some cases, there is no right or wrong way, but rather the way that works best using the tools you have. Another consideration is how much time you want to devote to making a structure. Some may just want to populate their railroads with buildings in quick order, while others don't mind spending hours building structures one board or shingle at a time. I am going to show you how to do both.

This book is based on a series of articles that I wrote for *Garden Railways* magazine. I realize that potential readers will have various levels of skill and commitment. The material in this book, for the most part, is geared toward beginners, but I have also included some advanced modeling techniques.

May 13, 1989, celebrated the golden spike day of the Crystal Springs Railroad. With the exception of the sawmill, the structures were all kits from companies such as Boom Town, Korber, Pola and Greenleaf. Many of these structures would eventually be replaced by scratchbuilt and some kitbashed buildings (combined or altered kits).

My only scratchbuilt structure in 1989 was my sawmill. The others were kits, such as the Scan-Kit engine house seen in the background.

This 1989 view shows an excellent, long-lasting model kit, Pola's water mill.

This 1989 photo shows a combination of plastic and wooden kits.

A kit like Bobby's garage is another high-quality product that can certainly be a permanent part of the railroad.

Part of the fun of populating your garden railway with structures is building each structure to represent the era and region you wish to model, and also building it as quickly or as carefully as you choose.

For example, the same building can be built with several techniques and materials to accomplish the same thing. One of the easiest and most realistic garden structures is a simple board-and-batten building.

This structure could be a simple box made of plywood or Masonite with battens and windows glued to it. This is not a structure that would last forever outdoors, but it is simple to make, would help your layout quickly, and requires few tools.

Another simple box could be made of plastic with battens glued on and ready-made plastic windows. This is a long-lasting structure and can be made to look realistic. See chapter 8.

A built-up frame with boards and battens applied individually with a shingled roof results in a very realistic-looking structure and can last a long time. See chapter 6.

This same structure also could be made using cast-resin parts. See chapter 11. This is a way to build a lot of structures quickly that will look both good and last a long time.

So just as there are many ways to construct a perfectly serviceable building, I hope this book will encourage you to consider many ways to accomplish your overall goals in your garden railway.

Most of all, I hope it will help you to realize you can do anything you set your mind to accomplish and have fun doing it.

CHAPTER 1

Plastic cement, glues, and adhesives

It's easy to be confused by the many plastic cements, glues, and adhesives available. Still it's very important to select the right one to get a good solid bond in your materials. This chapter covers the range of glues you'll need.

Many years ago, a friend of mine who was getting started in the hobby asked me what kind of glue he should use to adhere wooden shingles to his water tank's roof. I suggested silicone. Thinking silicone was too expensive, he used white glue instead. In about three weeks, every shingle fell off. Fortunately, the bond was so poor, he was able to clean up the glue residue and re-attach the shingles with silicone. It has been several years and the silicone has held.

Many types of common glues such as hot glue, white glue, and carpenter's glue are fine for indoor use but are not suitable for outdoors. You need a waterproof (not water-resistant) glue.

Plastic cement, glues, and adhesives and their correct applications are important subjects. Using the wrong one will lead to failure and frustration. Making the right selection will guarantee many years of service. There are an overwhelming number of choices of cement, glues, and adhesives. There is no one type that will work the "best" in every application, and because of the number of products available, it can become confusing. For practical reasons, I will limit my discussion to the most widely available products best suited to garden-railroad structures.

Wood to wood

Let's look at one of the most common materials used in garden railroading: wood. Wood-to-wood bonding for the outdoors is straightforward. For years I have used Titebond II wood glue, and it has served me well. Titebond III, an improved formula, is also available. I have used both, but I find that Titebond II is slightly thicker and less likely to run. There are similar glues made by other manufacturers, but I have not used them so I can't make any recommendations. When choosing a wood glue, make sure it says "waterproof" on the label. Note: The wood must be dry when it is glued. If the wood is wet, it will not bond properly.

Plastic to plastic

The cements used in assembling styrene or ABS plastic kits are solvent type. MEK (methyl ethyl ketone) is the active ingredient in most solvent-based glues used for these materials. It can be used in its purest form on styrene and ABS. MEK is available where paint is sold. It is a water-thin liquid, and can be applied using a syringe applicator or a brush. MEK is also useful as a paint remover and cleaning solvent. I have used it to remove printed lettering. It has powerful fumes, so use it in a well-ventilated area, and heed the warnings on the label.

Acrylic needs a special cement that is methylene chloride based. Don't use

Titebond III and Titebond II (not shown) are waterproof glues. They work well for joining wood to wood. Wood should be dry before applying. The glue becomes waterproof when it dries.

MEK (methyl ethyl ketone) is the active ingredient in most solvent-based plastic glues.

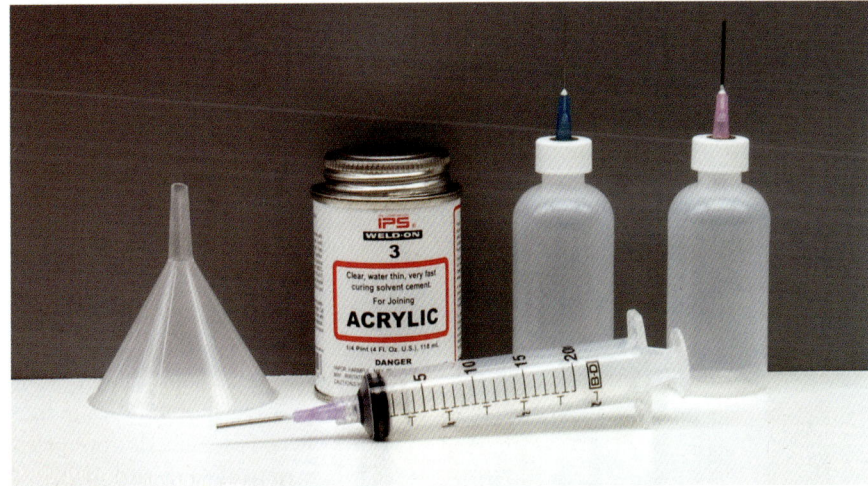

Water-thin cements can be applied to your work with a syringe bottle (right). The two bottles show different syringe tips. The smaller tip is more precise and easier to control. The large tip provides a higher flow for bigger projects.

methylene chloride by itself; it evaporates too quickly. This cement is very thin and can be applied using a syringe applicator or a brush. Like MEK, methylene chloride adhesive fumes are strong and hazardous, so use the glue in a well-ventilated area and heed the label warnings.

Here's a summary of some of my favorite solvent-type plastic cements:

IPS makes several variants of its Weld-On cements. Weld-On 3 is a clear, thin, fast-curing solvent cement for acrylic. Weld On 4 is also a clear, thin, fast-curing solvent cement for acrylic, but this formula has an additional agent that slows the curing time a bit by slowing the evaporation rate.

Weld-On 2007 is a clear, thin, fast-curing solvent cement for rigid vinyl

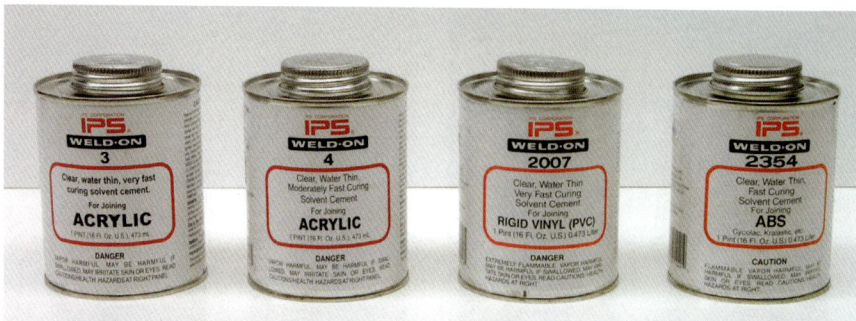

IPS Weld-On 3, Weld-On 4, Weld-On 2007, and Weld-On 2354 are solvent-type cements specifically designed for various plastics.

Using a syringe bottle

Here's a tip on how professionals use a syringe bottle to apply water-thin cements. First, fill the bottle nearly full of cement. Then, with the syringe pointing up, squeeze the bottle with your fingers until the excess air is expelled. While keeping your fingers in the depressed position, turn the bottle upside down. The vacuum you created will keep the cement in the bottle. To apply, squeeze the bottle. This method takes some practice, but once mastered, this will become your preferred type of application.

A pour spout and a funnel are one way to transfer the cement from the large can to the application bottle. Another way is to use the pump type syringe, shown on page 7.

IPS 16 bonds acrylic by a solvent-welding process. It is like syrup and runs freely, so an applicator tip (between the tubes) is recommend when applying. This solvent is also good for gluing styrene.

plastics (such as PVC) and Weld-On 2354 is a clear, thin, fast-curing solvent cement for ABS plastics.

IPS Weld-On 16 is the same type of glue as those listed above but it's more syrup-like in consistency. This product is fairly easy to work with and works best for adhering small parts such as trim pieces. Weld-On also contains MEK so it bonds acrylic and styrene. This is the best all-around cement for styrene and acrylic and should be in everyone's tool box.

Plastic Weld is Plastruct's brand of solvent cement, while Evergreen recommends Testor's liquid plastic cement.

Glue for Styrofoam

To glue Styrofoam, you should use a water-based contact cement such as 3M's Fastbond Contact Cement. The contact cement is applied to both mating surfaces, allowed to dry, then pressed together. Other types of glue will not dry as well, since the Styrofoam blocks the air. Fastbond can also be used to glue other materials to Styrofoam, such as wood.

CA cement

CA stands for cyanoacrylate ester. This is commonly called Super Glue, a trademarked name for one brand of CA. It can be used to glue plastic, wood, metal, leather, cloth, and your fingers (either together or to your project). CA cement is most useful for gluing together dissimilar materials, and it provides a quick bond.

To prevent CA from sticking to your skin, you can apply a product such as "Glove Cote" to your hands. If you are unfortunate enough to get glue on your skin, a product called de-bonder is available that will dissolve the glue. De-bonder is designed to dissolve CA joints.

CA glues are available in different formulas and viscosities. Different brands give them varying names, but the four basic types include:

1. Instant (or thin)—this is water thin and flows freely. The capillary effect will cause this glue to run into all spaces. This glue is tricky to apply. It's easy to use too much and it can be difficult to control. It is best to try a few practice pieces before using it on an actual project.
2. Gap-filling—this CA is thicker and is designed to bond joints that are not completely tight or have small gaps. This is the formula I use to glue resin walls together. This glue is easier to apply since it does not run.
3. Slow—this is an even thicker formula than the gap-filling version.
4. Gel—the thickest formula. This is one of the recommended products for gluing Precision Board.

An accelerator is a chemical that comes in a spray bottle or in an aerosol can. When sprayed on a CA-glue joint, it causes the cement to set instantly. This is big advantage in that it allows you to quickly cure your glue joints without clamping.

Cyanoacrylate adhesive (CA glue), commonly called "super glue," comes in several viscosities.

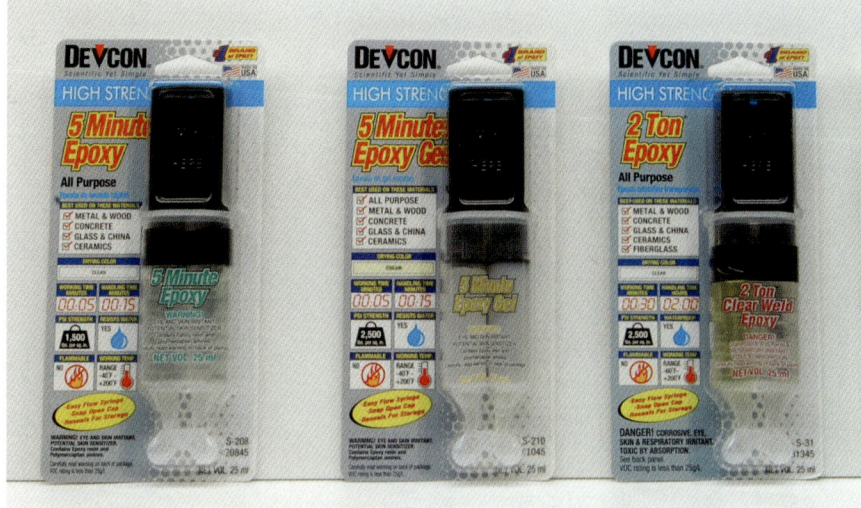

Devcon offers several types of epoxies. Be sure to read the information on the package to ensure the formula you choose is the right one for the job. Devcon offers its product in a convenient dispenser that measures out the correct amounts of parts A and B.

When using CA on plastic windows, there will sometimes be a chemical reaction that causes a white film to form on the plastic. There is a non-fogging formula of CA available. There are also special formulas of CA glue available for other materials such as for engineering plastic (such as Delrin). For more information on CA glues, visit the Super Glue website (www.supergluecorp.com/).

Keep in mind that CA is not waterproof, so CA joints need to be protected from the weather. Although CA will bond just about anything and is convenient to use, there are sometimes other choices available. For example CA will glue styrene to styrene, but a better choice would be a cement designed for styrene such as IPS No. 16. CA glue should be your second choice in most cases.

Epoxy

Epoxy is a two-part glue that is mixed immediately before use. There are dozens of epoxy formulas on the market. Be sure to read the label to see if a particular epoxy will work with the material you are bonding. Curing time ranges from quick to extra slow. The slower formulas usually are the strongest. In most cases, the project will have to be clamped while the epoxy is curing.

In general, epoxy does not include solvents. This eliminates possible damage that might be caused by solvent-based products that may attack painted finishes.

Epoxy is a little difficult to work with. Its viscosity before curing is similar to honey. This is not my favorite glue to work with because of the mixing and slower curing times, but it is good where maximum mechanical bonding strength is required. It is available at hobby shops, automotive-parts shops, and hardware and home-improvement stores.

Epoxy can be colored with pigments and used to fix cracks.

A toothpick can be used to apply the mixed epoxy to small parts. It can also be applied into the crack, then sanded smooth once it's cured.

Below are a few types of epoxies that are available from Devcon with their information and key features.

Five-minute epoxy and epoxy gel

Five-minute epoxy is a rapid-curing, general-purpose adhesive/encapsulant which easily dispenses and mixes in seconds. It dries in 15 minutes with full strength in one hour.

Key features:
- Bonds rigid durable materials such as metals, glass, ceramics, concrete, and wood in all combinations
- Forms a clear, hard, rigid bond
- It self-levels in minutes
- Functional cure in 1 hour
- 100% reactive, no solvents

The gel version is a thixotropic/non-migrating gel adhesive with excellent gap-filling properties. Its bonding strength is almost twice as strong as regular five-minute epoxy. This my favorite epoxy and should be in everyone's tool box. Features include:
- High tensile strength (2,500 psi)
- Good solvent resistance to gas, oil, and other solvents
- Non sagging, which makes it ideal for use on vertical surfaces
- Excellent gap-filling qualities without tremendous shrinkage
- Fast curing for bond tags on machinery and equipment

Two-ton epoxy

This is an extremely strong water-resistant epoxy adhesive that forms a powerful bond with ferrous and non-ferrous metals, ceramics, wood, concrete, or glass in any combination.

Key features:
- Medium-cure adhesive which produces non-shrinking, rigid bonds
- Fills poorly mated joining surfaces while providing excellent adhesion
- Water-resistant
- Good impact resistance
- Can be used to encapsulate parts

Epoxy is also available in putty/clay form. This will be covered in its own chapter on Magic Sculpt. See photo 8.

Plastic welder (acrylic based)

This is a tough, fast-curing acrylic-based structural adhesive with superior impact and peel resistance to most

Plastic Welder is a strong glue that can bond a large variety of plastics.

Quick Grip is an adhesive that can be used to bond a variety of dissimilar materials.

plastic surfaces such as ABS, PVC, composite polyesters, polycarbonate, PET (what two-liter plastic bottles are made of), fiber glass, wood, concrete, ceramic, and metal. This product does contain a strong solvent.

Key Features
- Requires minimal surface preparation
- Bonds dissimilar substrates as well as unprepared metals, ceramics, wood, and standard engineered plastics
- Functional cure in one hour
- Final bond is resistant to weathering, humidity, and wide variations of temperature
- 1:1 formula for easy dispensing
- Good gap-filling capabilities.

Omni-Stick (Quick Grab)

Omni-Stick, the brand name of the product formerly known as Quick Grab, is a contact cement made by Precision Products. It dries clear and is easier to use on smaller parts than silicone, but is more expensive. Omni-Stick is available at hobby shops and miniatures/dollhouse shops.

Silicone

Silicone is generally marketed as caulk. These products are available at hardware stores, home-improvement stores, and automotive-parts stores. You can buy silicone in small tubes similar to toothpaste tubes, or in a larger tube designed to be used in a caulking gun. A caulking gun is useful for applying silicone over joints. Once the tube is open, the product should be used as soon as possible. Opened tubes will eventually dry out.

There are two types of silicone caulking. One is pure silicone, such as General Electric Silicone II. In this form it is not paintable; in fact, it will repel water-based paints. You can, however, paint the surface ahead of time if you want a paint color in the area you are gluing. You could also apply a thin coat of paintable silicone over the pure silicone.

Pure silicone is available in colors. You can buy clear, brown, white, aluminum, and black. Clear can be used around windows or where you want an invisible glue joint. Brown can be used for gluing natural wood, and aluminum or black silicone can be used to glue down metal roofing material. It will adhere to just about anything—wood, glass, resin, cloth, paper—and it remains flexible.

This material is messy to work with and is very difficult to use on small details. Cleanup is difficult, too; you must wait for it to cure and then peel it off. The best use of this material is as an adhesive for roofing materials and for inside joints where painting is not an issue.

The second form of the material, siliconized caulk, is paintable and easier to clean up, but is not as strong or flexible as pure silicone. It is less expensive and easier to spread, though. This type of silicone is better on wood; I would not use it on resins or plastic.

Acrylic-latex caulk is another choice. It shares the strength characteristics of siliconized caulks. It can be cleaned up with water, and you can wet your finger and work the material into small areas, which is an advantage. Acrylic-latex caulk can also be used to glue smaller parts since overflow can be cleaned up with water.

Note: Not all pure silicones are the same. Some have better adhesion properties. In general, less expensive versions don't work as well for our intended purposes. The less-expensive brand may work better in your bathroom or kitchen because it has mold inhibiters and it is intended to be used as caulking, but it may not have a strong bond. I use General Electric Silicone II and have had good luck with it.

3M Marine Fast Cure 5200 Adhesive Sealant

This is a high-performance polyurethane that becomes tack free in one hour and fully cures in approximately 24 hours. The seal is extremely strong, and it retains strength above or below the water line. It remains flexible, and has excellent resistance to weathering and salt water. It's also easy to apply with a manual caulking gun.

E-6000

This is adhesive has been call "the second best thing to glue anything," meaning there is usually a specific glue for certain materials that is the best, but E-6000 will glue anything. This is a flexible adhesive, and it's useful for adhering large dissimilar surfaces.

The only drawback to this product is its working characteristics. It is similar to working with silicone, but it tends to flow and self level. You do not want to touch it, because it is a sticky gel-type glue. A tip for using this glue is to warm it prior to use. Run the tube under some hot water or place it in the sun. This will soften the material and allow it to flow more freely. When using E-6000 from a tube, it is recommended that you use an extension nozzle to allow you to apply the adhesive accurately. It is important to clamp the parts being glued.

This glue tends to squeeze out of the joint. The secret to using this adhesive is to resist the temptation to remove the excess right away. Touching it prematurely will only spread it around, causing a mess. If you let it cure for at least one hour but not more than 24 hours, you can remove the excess by peeling it away as it is flexible at this point. This will leave a clean joint.

E-6000 is a professional product and the one I am most familiar with. Similar products to E-6000 are Shoe Goo, Goop, and Marine Goop, all made by the same company that makes E-6000. Visit the company's Web site at: eclecticproduct.com (Amazinggoop.com).

Adhesive on a roll

The material I'm referring to is called "Killer Red" by Bron Tape. It is not actually tape. It has no material in it such as such as cloth or plastic; it is just adhesive on a roll. The adhesive is on a red carrier that is peeled away once the first side is stuck down. Another supplier of a similar material is Johnson Plastics. They refer to their materials as "Pressure sensitive adhesive," available in sheets, in tape form, or on a roll. 3M offer a similar product called VHB Tape.

Advantages:
- It is very strong.
- Because it is in a tape or sheet form, it applies cleanly and neatly.
- It can be cut to just the right size, so there is no oozing when it is applied.
- There is no drying time; it bonds on contact.
- It is weather proof.
- You can bond almost anything to anything but it works best on smooth surfaces such as plastic and metal.
- It can be cut with a scissors or a hobby knife.

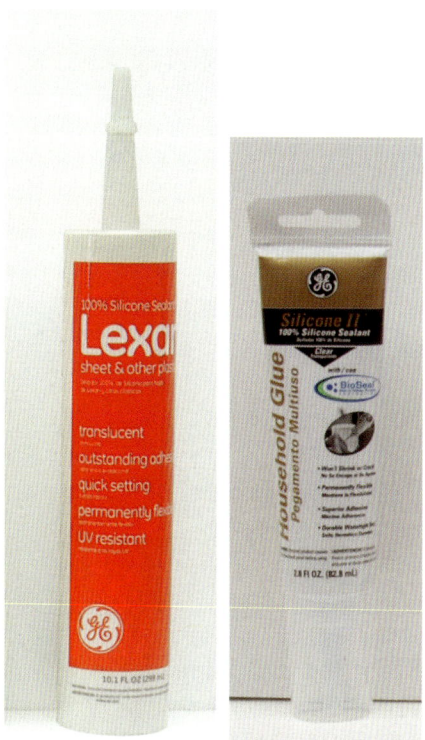

Silicone sealant performs well as an adhesive in many applications.

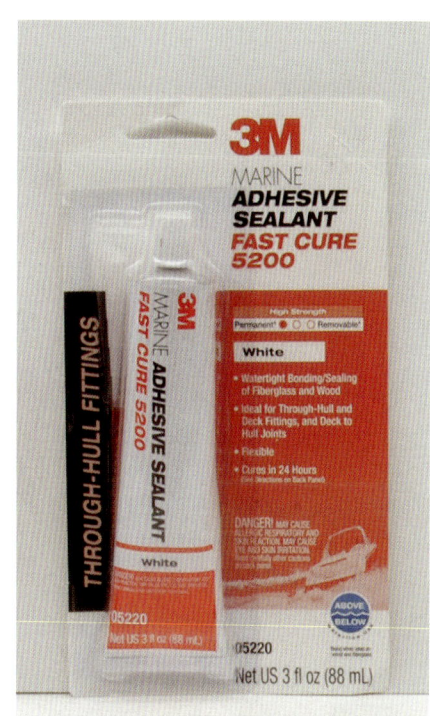

3M Marine Fast Cure 5200 Adhesive Sealant is available in a small tube with an applicator cap.

E-6000 is available in both the small tubes shown here and caulking gun tubes. If you buy the small tube, an applicator nozzle, sold separately, is recommended. E-6000 comes in clear, white, or black.

Please note that this material is not gap filling like foam tape. It won't work for items that have a rough or uneven surface, such as taping down a circuit board.

The bond is strongest when adhering smooth materials such as acrylic, metal, and glass. It can be used to bond wood, but the wood must be dust free and relatively smooth. For example, if you bonded rough-cut wood, the bond would not be as strong due to the loose wood fibers. The adhesive will stick to the fibers, but the fibers can be pulled away from the parent piece. Sanding rough wood will give you a better bond. Sanding and sealing the wood will also greatly improve the holding power.

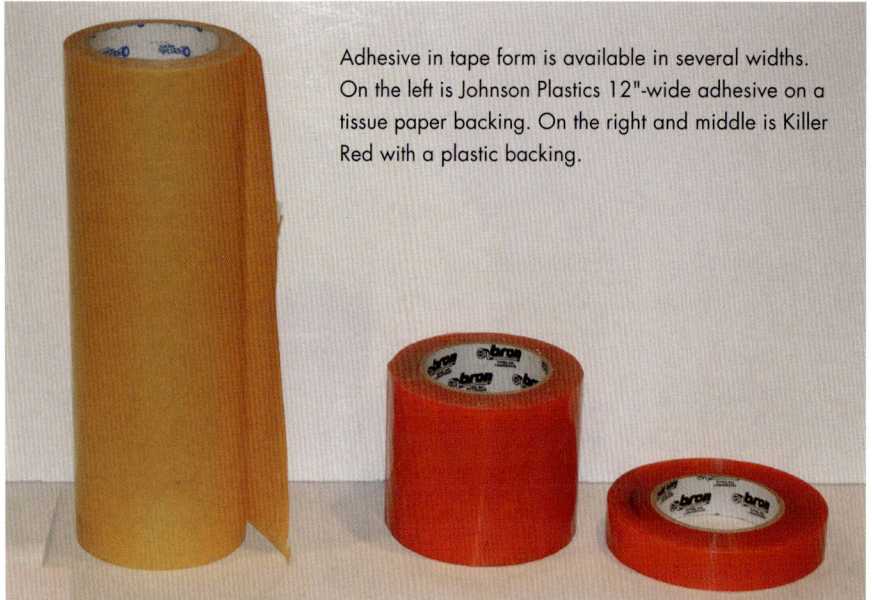

Adhesive in tape form is available in several widths. On the left is Johnson Plastics 12"-wide adhesive on a tissue paper backing. On the right and middle is Killer Red with a plastic backing.

SOURCES

Bron Tape Northern California
29430 Union City Blvd.
Union City, CA 94587
800-782-8973
510-429-1980

Available in tape form .008" thick on rolls in a variety of widths. It has a polypropylene film carrier. Note: Bron has a $100 minimum order policy.

Johnson Plastics
Minneapolis, Minn.
800-869-7800

Pressure sensitive adhesive 4mm acrylic adhesive.

Roll: T-330-12
        12" x 55 yds.
        Tissue carrier
Sheet: SHT330
        18" x 24"
        Polyester carrier
Tape: T329
        size ½" x 55 yds.
        Tissue carrier
Tape: T3291
        size 1" x 55 yds.
        Tissue carrier

Tap plastics
www.tapplastics.com

ITW Devcon
30 Endicott St.
Danvers, MA 01923
Technical Service: 800-933-8266
Customer Service: 800-626-7226
www.devcon.com

Pacer Products
9420 Santa Anita Ave.
Rancho Cucamonga, CA 91730
800-538-3091
www.supergluecorp.com

3M offers adhesive on smaller rolls for consumer use.

Glue runs, smudges, and oozing can ruin an otherwise great model. This is especially a problem with windows. If you wish to glue glass to plastic or metal, you could use CA, silicone, epoxies, or Goop. While all of these will bond glass to metal, every one of them is hard to work with. It is difficult if not impossible to use these adhesives without making a mess. If you use a pressure-sensitive adhesive, it will give you a clean finish. You can precut the tape to the size you need. Apply the tape to one side and simply press the parts together. An instant bond with no mess!

Another method of using this adhesive for attaching small strip material, such as window mullions, is to cut the tape into thin strips the same width as the strip materials that you are going top attach. For Killer Red, it is easiest to use a hobby knife. I like to roll out the tape and stick it down to a discarded piece of carrier so I can place the tape on a cutting surface.

Killer Red and Johnson Plastic pressure-sensitive adhesive

Killer Red is a stronger and slightly thicker product. It has a polypropylene film carrier, which makes it a little harder to cut by hand. It is only available in tape form. It is my first choice for smaller parts since strength is more important when you have less surface area.

Johnson Plastics' pressure-sensitive adhesive is thinner and a little easier to cut. It is available in 18" x 24" sheets, in tape form (either ½" or 1" widths), or on a 12"-wide, 55-yard-long roll. It is my first choice for attaching sheet material since strength is not as critical due to the larger mounting surface. The roll has a tissue carrier, which I find easier to cut.

Both materials can be cut with scissors or a hobby knife with a No. 11 or equivalent blade. Both materials tend to foul the scissors if the adhesive gets on the blade. This happens when the material is cut with the scissors at an angle other then about 90 degrees to the adhesive. It takes a little practice to perfect the cutting technique. For intricate projects, I would use Johnson Plastics pressure-sensitive adhesive and the hobby knife since it is easier to cut.

Tools

> For the purpose of this book, I will assume that you own household tools such as a hammer, screwdrivers, pliers, and diagonal cutters. This discussion will be about tools specifically for miniature-model building.

CHAPTER 2

There is a saying that "A craftsman is only as good as his tools." While tools are no substitute for imagination and skill, good tools can certainly make life easier. You don't need a room full of tools to get started, but there are certain tools that you must have as a beginner. As your skills grow and you build more projects, you can expand your tool inventory by getting some of the nice-to-have tools. Eventually, if your interest continues to grow, you can buy some of the dream tools—the ones that take you beyond the average.

Having a wide variety of appropriate tools at your disposal makes it easier to build more accurately. The result will be realistic structures you will be proud of.

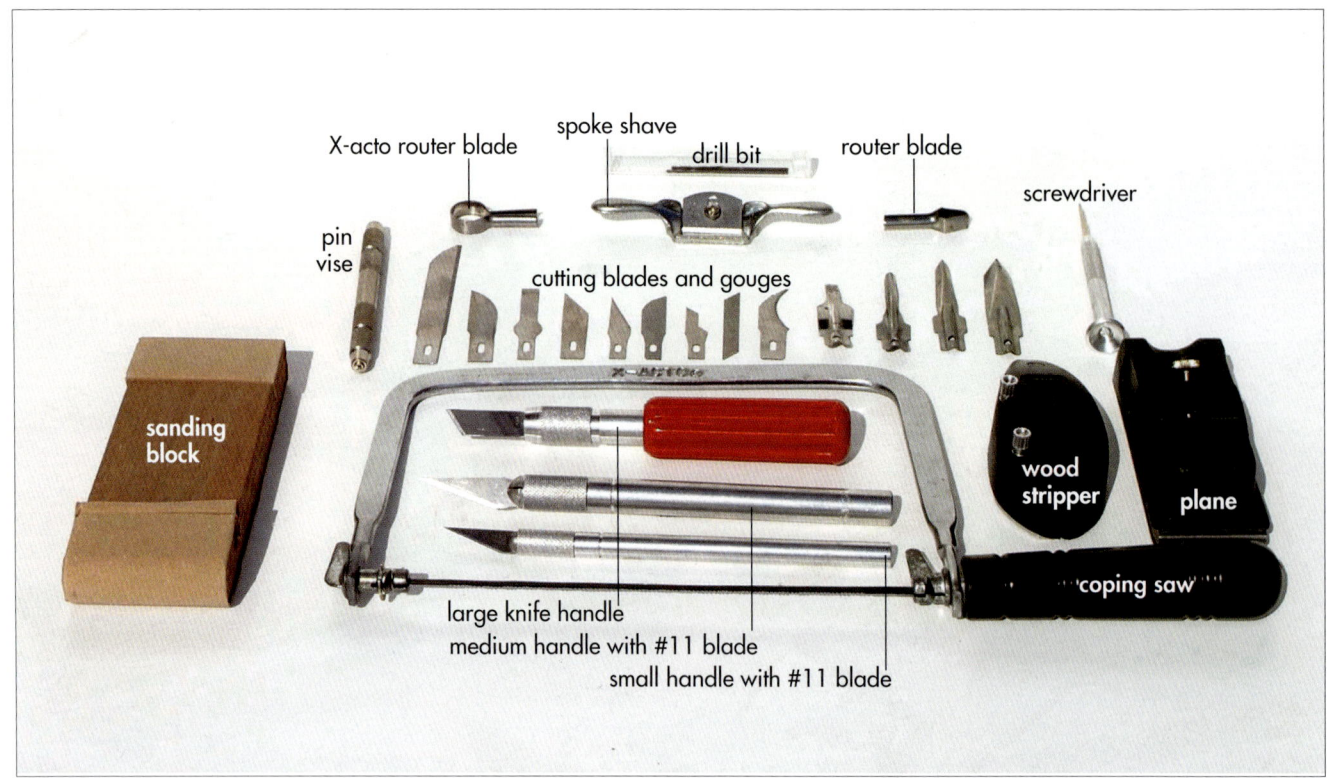

X-acto tools. The most-used tool in my workshop is a basic hobby knife. I use an X-acto brand (there are others) knife with a No. 11 blade. This tool is like an extra hand. I use it for everything from cutting and peeling backing material to picking up small wooden parts. Along with the basic handle, I keep a 100-pack of replacement blades on hand. If you are just getting started, a basic X-acto starter set is good choice. This photo shows many other tools, including a sanding block, pin vise, a variety of cutting blades and gouges, spoke shave, router blade, drill bits, screwdriver, wood stripper, coping saw, small and medium knife handles with No. 11 blades, and a large handle and larger blade.

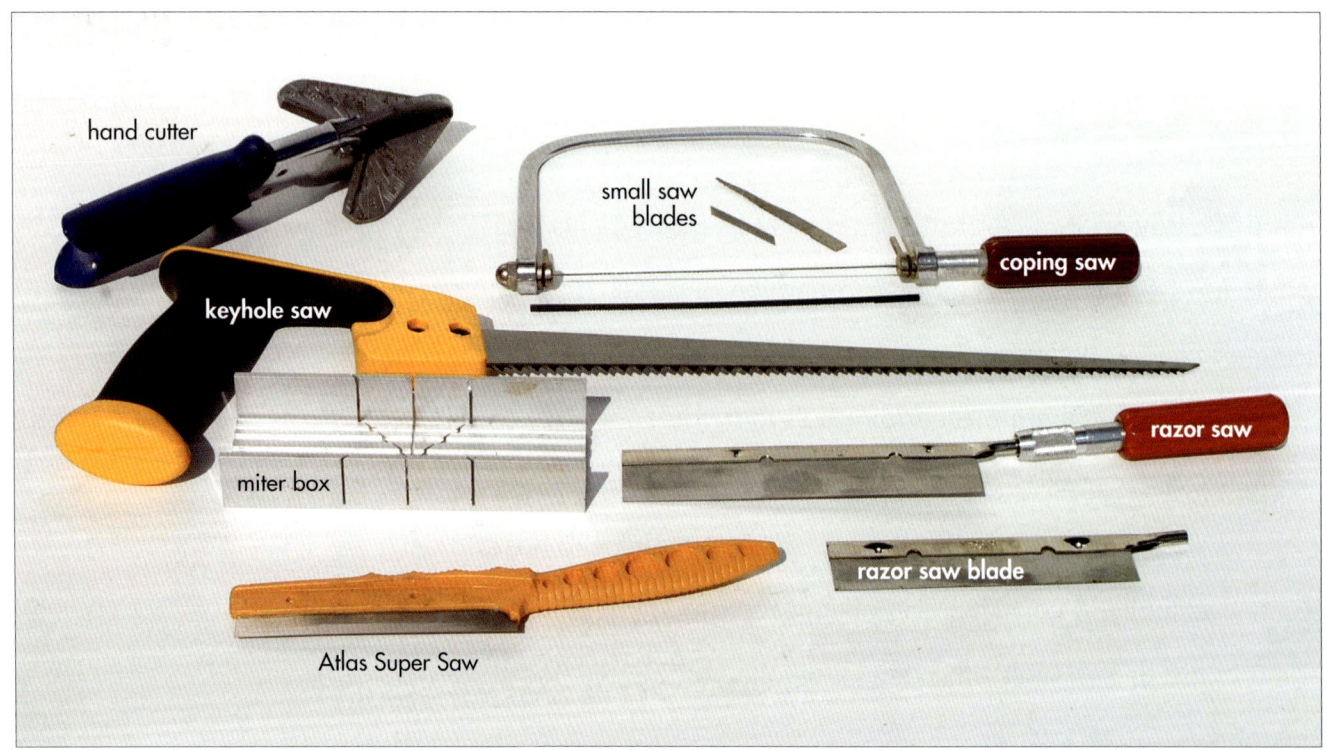

Saws. You'll find many different cutting tools handy in building structures. A hand cutter works well for strip material. A coping saw is an old-time hand tool that is a must for interior cutting and fretwork and useful for cutting window and door openings in plywood, Masonite, and plastics. A variety of cutting blades are available. A hole must be drilled to give the saw access to the material when doing interior cuts. Inside the coping saw are two small saw blades designed to fit into an X-acto knife handle. These are good for clean-up cuts and trimming hard-to-reach areas. A keyhole saw is handy for interior cuts. This is hefty tool, although not as accurate as a coping saw.

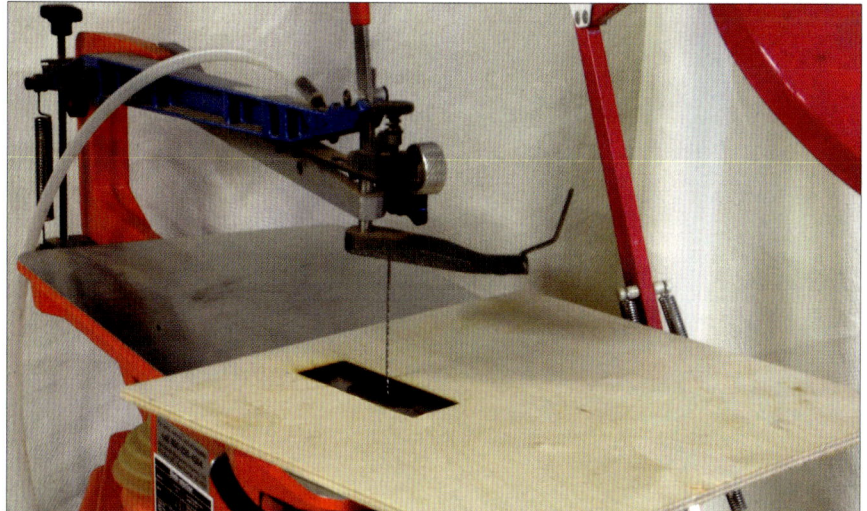

Miter box and razor saw. A razor saw can be used with or without a miter box. The miter box is helpful for cutting trim materials.

Saws and cutting tools

There are as many saws as there are materials from which you can build things. When I first started making models, I used a basic hand saw and a coping saw. Later, I bought a Dremel Motoshop. This tool came with several attachments such as a disc sander and flexible shaft that held a variety of rotary tips. This was a compact tool and was an excellent starter set. The original Motoshop is long out of production but there are several modern versions of this tool available. These combination tools are great for beginners.

Jig saw. This is a power saw where the blade protrudes downward. This saw is similar to a scroll saw, but it's not as accurate, mainly because you have to move the saw rather than the work piece. It is also more difficult to see the work surface as you are cutting. The jig saw's main advantage is that you do not have to disassemble the saw for interior cuts.

Scroll saw. A scroll saw is basically a powered version of a coping saw. Its advantage is speed. It can cut through materials quickly and accurately. A variety of cutting blades are available. For inside cuts, like windows and doors, drill a hole into the material, disconnect the blade and insert it into the hole, and then re-connect the blade back to the saw. A couple of disadvantages are this tool can vibrate the work piece if it not held down firmly by the operator. The blade moves too fast for cutting styrene so will melt the plastic, trapping the blade in the work. It is not intended for straight cuts, as it is difficult to control.

Mini chop saw. A large chop saw (not shown) is useful for cutting larger pieces of wood, but it's dangerous for cutting small strips of wood. A mini chop saw is a great tool for cutting small strip wood. The one shown has a 2" blade. I made my own table extension. This allows me to set up stops for duplicating parts. This saw can cut wood, plastic, and brass.

Chopper. The Chopper by NorthWest Short Line is used to cut wood or plastic strip material to length. It is good for making duplicate parts. The cutting arm holds a single-edge razor blade. Materials are placed in position on the table, then the arm is pushed down, cutting the material. A fence and a positioning block hold the material being cut to ensure a straight edge.

Table saw

A 10" standard table saw can be used for making model lumber, but it is somewhat tricky and you must use great caution when trying to mill small pieces of wood.

When milling miniature lumber, you must use a zero-clearance throat plate, which will prevent the wood from falling down into the saw. If your saw cannot be fitted with a zero-clearance throat plate, clamp a piece of plywood or Masonite hardboard on top of the table, with the blade lowered. Turn on the saw and ease the blade up through the Masonite. This will give you a zero-clearance cutting table. Use your original fence by placing the Masonite alongside it before raising the blade, or create your own fence by using a straightedge made of hard wood or metal, using a T-square to align the fence. This is an accurate way to cut miniature lumber.

A set of gauges can be bought or made. These are brass pieces that are the correct sizes for the cuts you want to make. Insert the gauge between the blade and the fence, square up the fence and blade, and begin cutting.

▶ A set of gauges can be made or purchased. These gauges are from Micro-Mark. The gauge helps in squaring up the fences, which is important for safety reasons. If the fence is not perfectly parallel to the blade, you could have kick-back.

Here's a table saw fitted with a zero-clearance plate in the form of a sheet of Masonite hardboard. The zero-clearance throat prevents the wood from falling down into the saw hole.

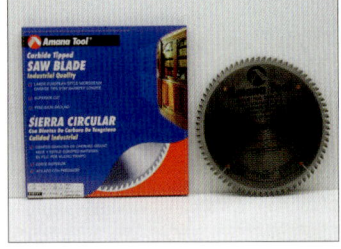

For cutting plastics such as acrylic, a special saw blade is recommended. Standard blades will chip plastic.

Thickness sander. This tool is designed to sand rough lumber to a specific thickness. Above is an example of a rough-cut "fence board" that has passed through the thickness sander. I also use this machine to finish the backsides of cast resin walls.

Duplicutter. The NorthWest Short Line Duplicutter is designed to hold sheet materials, such as plastics and thin wood, in place while being cut. The material is placed against the alignment plate. A bar is placed over the material, holding it in place while you score or cut it. Since the alignment plate is locked in place, you can use this tool to make duplicate parts.

Brad gun, Pin nailer. Above is an 18-gauge brad gun, available in either electric or pneumatic (shown) types. This is a must-have for making structures such as trestles. A brad has a small T head and is likely to split small-sized lumber. Below is a pin nailer. This tool shoots very small pins having no heads. A pin nailer is an excellent tool for attaching small pieces of wood. Certain techniques must be used when using a pin nailer. These will be covered in more detail in the chapter on building wooden buildings.

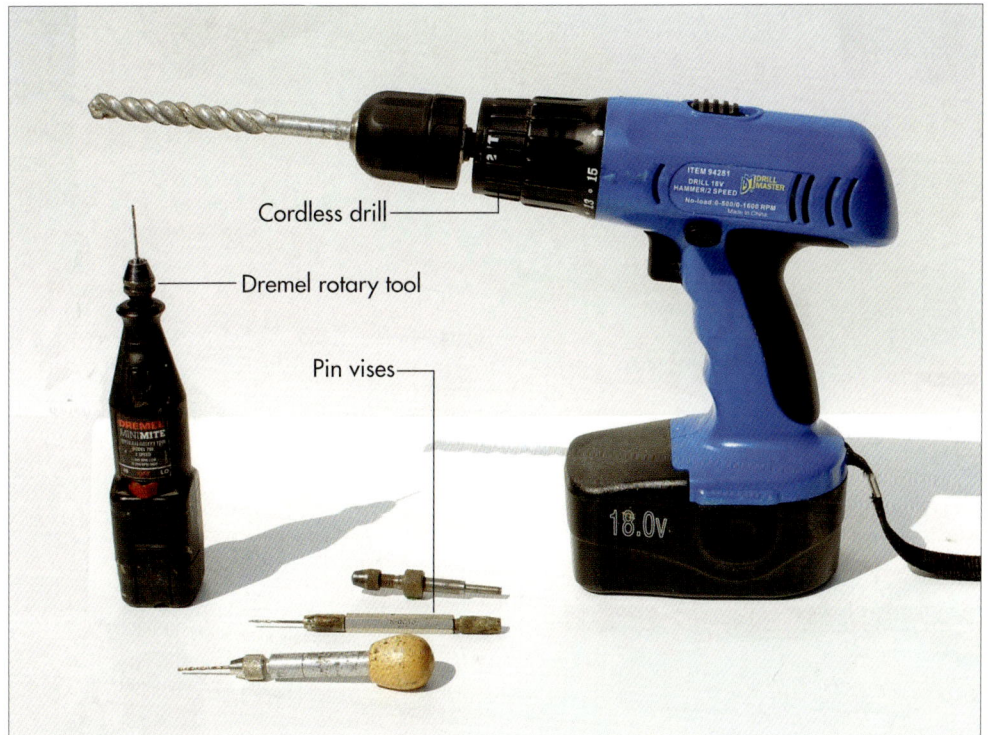
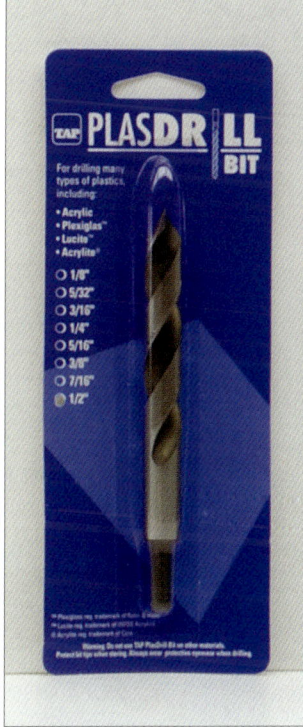

Drills. A drill press (not shown) is a convenient tool to have on hand. It is especially useful to drill pilot holes in combination with a scroll saw to cut window holes. However, for convenience, a cordless drill is a handy tool to have in your workshop. A large 18-volt drill is useful for drilling pilot holes and even for drilling though cement (such as when making bases for your structures). Dremel makes a cordless drill for drilling small holes. Also shown are several pin vises, hand-powered drills that are useful for drilling small holes. At right is a special plastic drill bit. Notice that the tip is angled more steeply than a common drill bit.

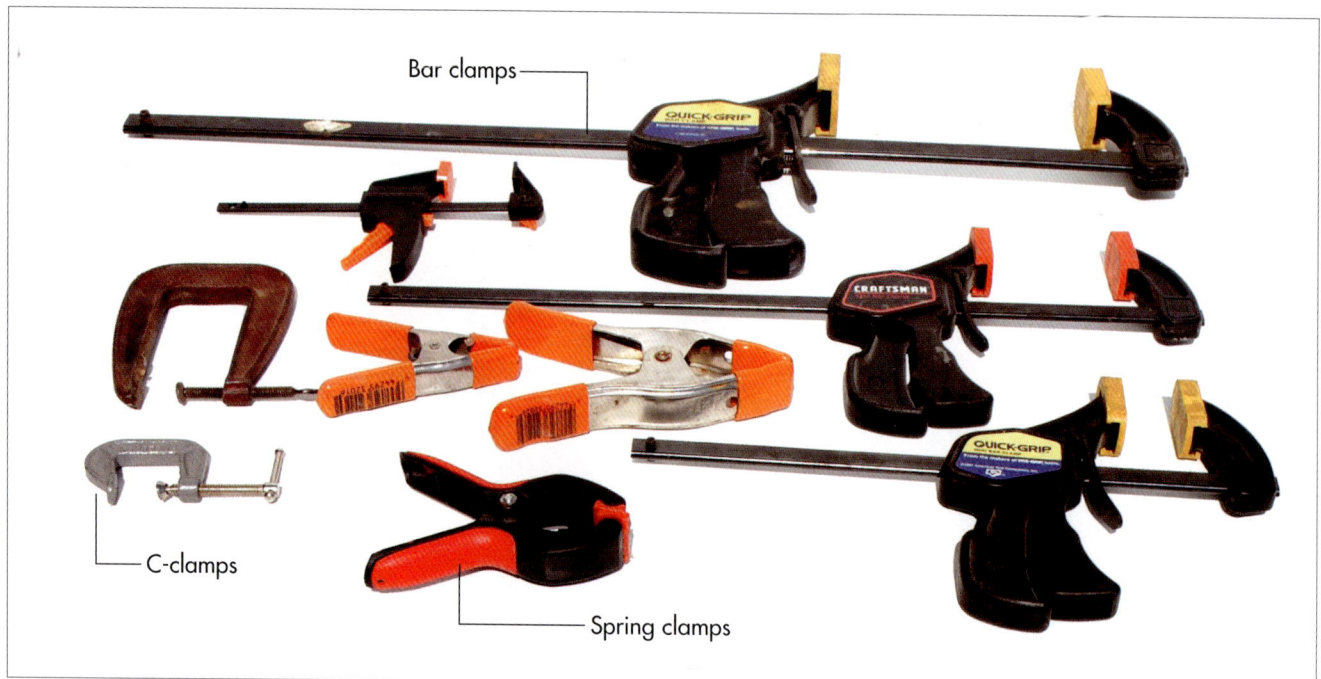

Clamps. Bar clamps, C-clamps, and spring clamps in various sizes are all helpful for holding things in place while gluing. You can also use clothespins and clamp-type paper clips.

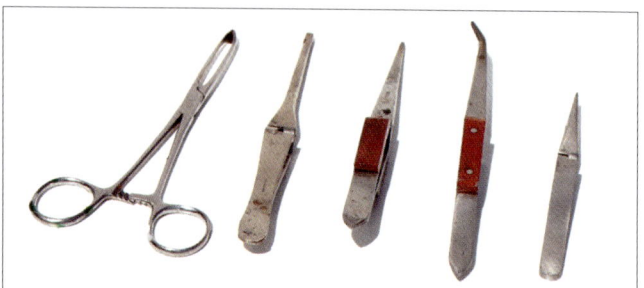

Tweezers. Locking tweezers are useful for holding parts in place or for handling small parts, especially while painting or gluing them.

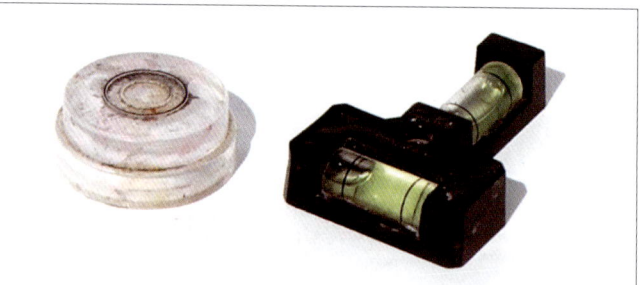

Special levels. A bulls-eye level and a two-plane level are used to level building bases.

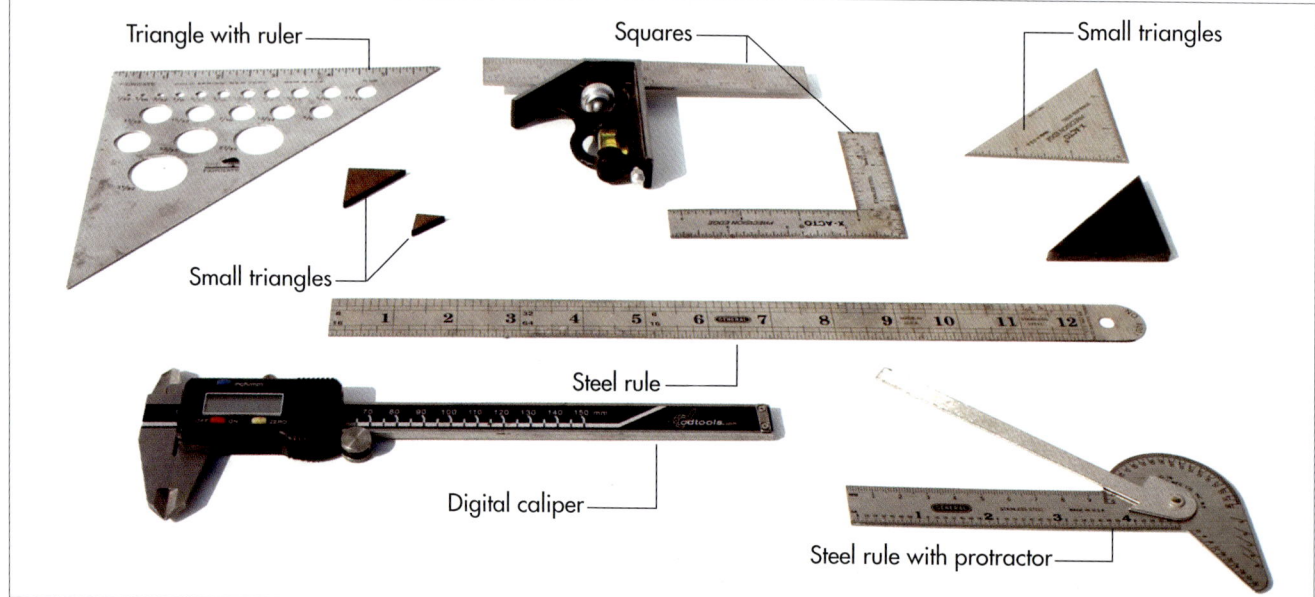

Measuring tools. Measuring and aligning parts accurately is important. Shown here are just a few tools that make this task possible. From upper left: a triangular square with hole gauge, small corner squares (used to align window and door frames), small combination square, small filled square, small corner squares, metal ruler, digital calipers, protractor.

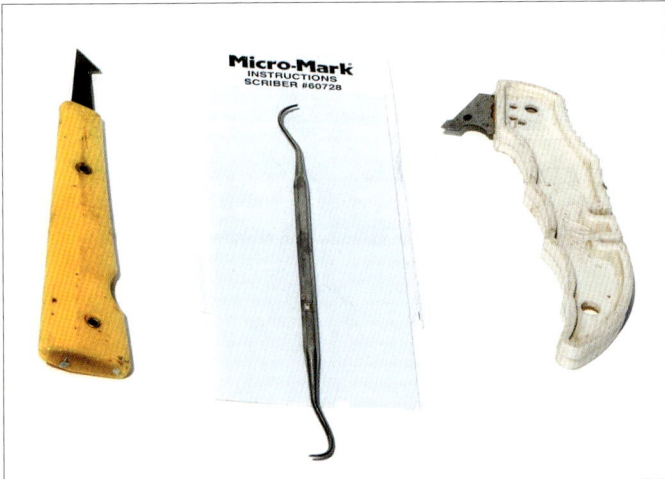 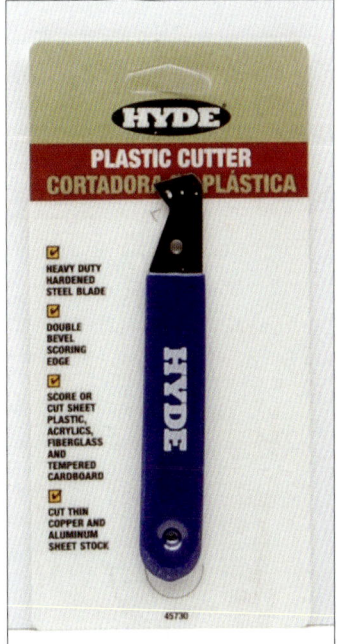 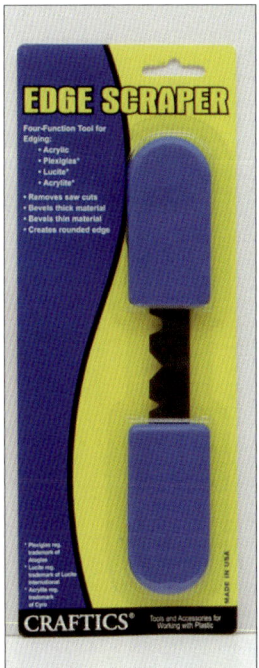

Scribes and cutters for plastic. It is best to cut plastic with tools designed to do so. Rather than cutting through the material, like a knife, these tools scribe the plastic. The tools on the right and left are specifically for cutting plastic; the center tool is a scribe used to create lines in plastic. The photo at near right is a heavy-duty plastic cutter, and the photo at far right shows a scraper used to clean up cut plastic edges.

Sanding tools. A combination disc and belt sander makes sanding quick and easy for medium-size jobs. For smaller and detailed sanding work, sanding blocks are useful. Shown here are (from left) a rubber cleaner designed to clean clogged sanding discs or belts, sliding sanding block used to accurately sand angled cuts, small sanding tools used to sand in tight areas, hard rubber general purpose sanding block with a both a flat and curved surface, shown with sandpaper on the flat side.

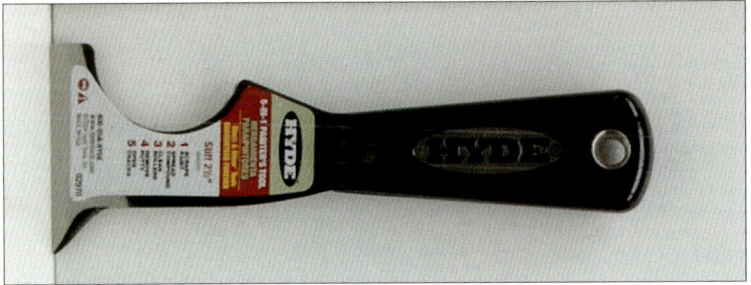

Scraper. A multipurpose scraper is useful for a variety of jobs, such as removing excess glue and adhesive.

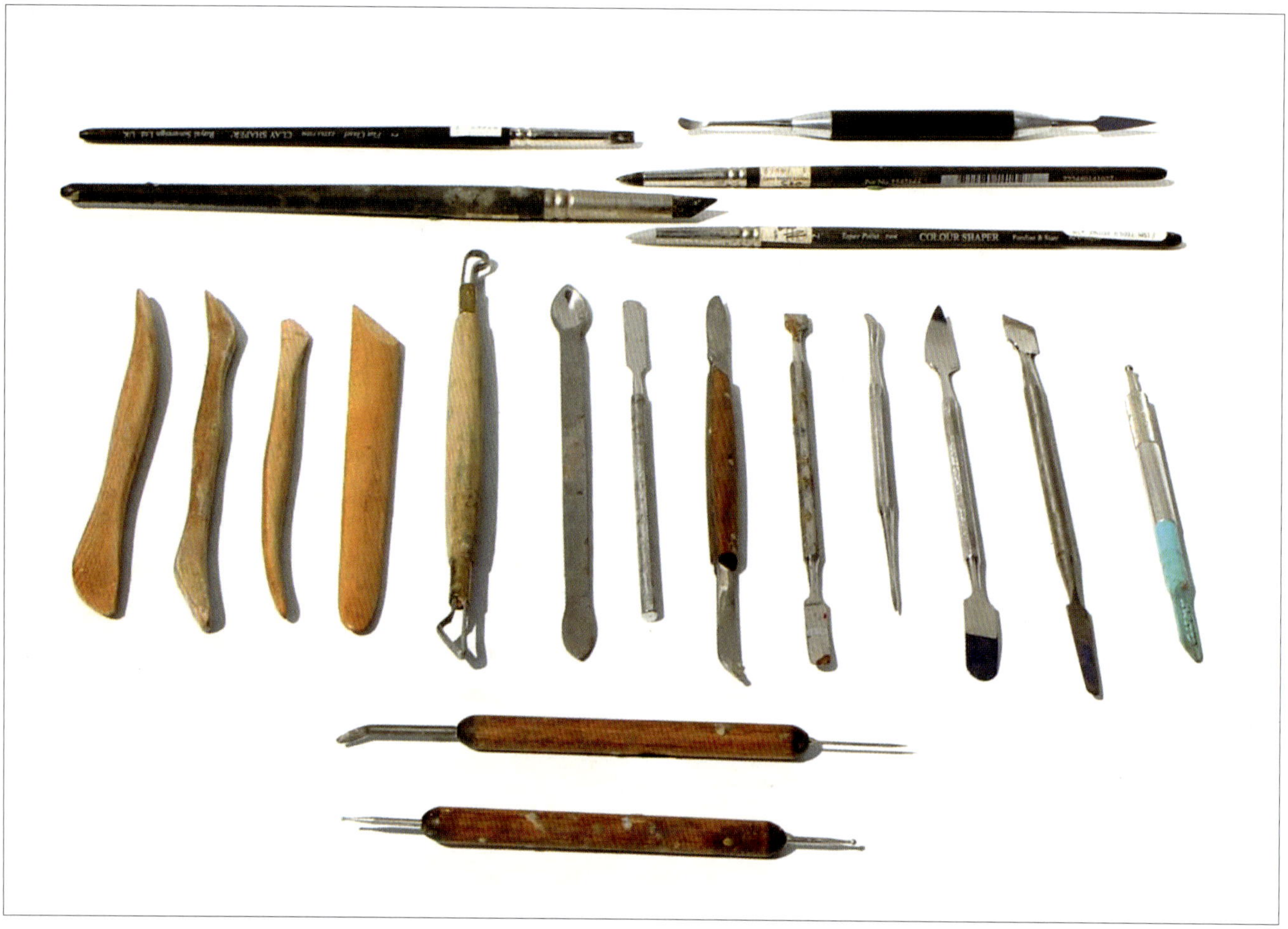

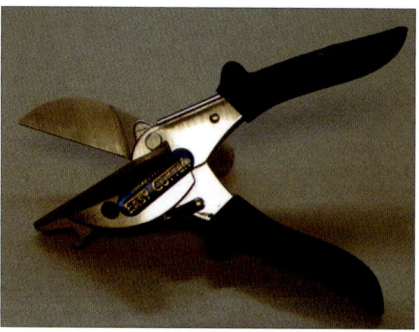

Sculpting tools. The variety of tools shown above can be used to sculpt materials like Magic Sculp, Sculpy, and Fimo.

◀ **Easy Cutter.** This is a handy tool for cutting strip materials and shingles. It cuts both plastic and wood. It is quick and easy to use but is not intended to be used for finish-type work.

▶ **Hot-wire cutters.** The Hot Wire Foam Factory is useful for cutting sheet Styrofoam. The large cutting table holds the cutting wire. You push the Styrofoam through, and the wire cuts by melting the foam. The wishbone is for freehand work like making Styrofoam scenery, and the pencil type tools are used for engraving lines into the foam.

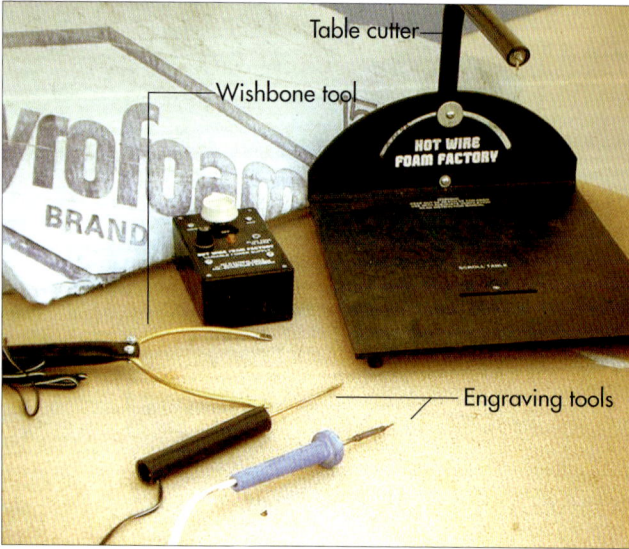

SOURCES

Dremel
www.dremel.com
800-436-3635

Hot Wire Foam Factory
216 East Laurel Ave.
Lompoc, CA 93436
www.hwff.com

NorthWest Short Line
Box 423
Seattle, WA 98111-0423
www.nwsl.com

X-acto products
Elmer's Products, Inc.
1 Easton Oval
Columbus, OH 43219
www.xacto.com/products.asp

Micro Mark
1-800-225-1066
Micromark.com

Kits

Many large-scale plastic structure kits are available today to help you quickly populate your railroad. For some modelers, these structures may be a starting point. For others, kits may be their ultimate goal. In either case, a plastic building kit offers you a structure that is weatherproof when properly assembled. Large-scale plastic kits generally fall into two categories—injection-molded styrene (such as Pola, Piko, and other brands) and cast polyurethane resin (Railroad Avenue, Muella Scale Models, and others).

CHAPTER 3

Kits allow you to populate your garden railway with structures in relatively short order. Many kits are available to represent depots, stores, and industries.

The church on Dart and Dot Rinefort's railroad in San Rafael, Calif., was kitbashed from Pola's St. Michael church. The building was shortened and the entrance modified with the addition of a stairway. Dart Rinefort photo

A Pola building receives silicone reinforcement in its joints. Silicone repels water and is tough, yet flexible, when dry.

Injection molded

Let's look at styrene plastic kits first. By and large these are well-engineered products, and when assembled according to directions, they should last many years outdoors.

The glue provided in the kits is generally very good. It forms a bond by melting or welding the plastic together. When assembling these kits, follow the manufacturer's instructions and use the provided glue. If glue is not provided, you must a use glue that's designed for styrene, such as IPD Weld-On 3, No. 16, or MEK. Glue for styrene actually welds the plastic by melting it together (see chapter 2).

Weld-On 3 and MEK are water-thin liquids that need to be applied with a syringe bottle or a small brush. When using water-thin glues, clamp or hold the parts together. Then, using the syringe, squeeze the glue so it flows into the joint. Capillary action will pull the glue into the joint. The glue can also be brushed into a joint. It will take a few minutes for the glue to form a bond. It must first soften the plastic, then melt the joints together. I like to use a brush to coat the joint just prior to assembly. Then use the syringe to apply glue to the joints. This speeds up the bonding process.

Once the walls and roof of the structure are together, add a bead of silicone to all interior joints. This is done with a caulking gun, on the inside of the building. Run a bead in each corner where the walls meet, along the edge where the walls and the roof meet, and then in the peak of the roof. Use a piece of wood or your finger to work the silicone into the joints. Silicone is messy, so you will want to wear gloves.

When the silicone cures, you'll have a building that is solid. In the case of styrene, the silicone is not intended to be the sole adhesive, as silicone does not adhere well to styrene. In this application, it is intended to seal the joint and act a reinforcing element.

I have found that gluing the roof in place adds structural integrity to the building. If you want the roof to be removable, I suggest gluing the corner braces either at the top edges of the walls or at the bottom edges, or in both places. This will give the building lateral support, which is especially helpful if you take your buildings indoors. Buildings have been known to collapse while being handled after they've spent time outside.

An alternate method of reinforcing styrene kits is to glue ¼"-square strip styrene into the corners with styrene-compatible cement. Styrene strips are available from Evergreen Scale Models, and are available at your local hobby shop.

There are a few "don'ts" in building styrene kits. Don't use CA glue! CA will bond the plastic and it will give you a seemingly strong joint, but in time it could come loose. I've learned this the hard way. When I first started assembling Pola kits I was in a hurry, so I used CA. I liked the idea of gluing a joint and zapping it with Zip Kicker for an instant bond. In time, the CA crystallized and the buildings fell apart. I had to scrape all of the CA residue off the joints, then to re-glue the building using a styrene cement.

Cast-resin buildings

Kits manufactured by companies like Railroad Avenue, Muella Scale Models, and makers of other craftsmen kits are made of polyurethane resin. This material cannot be welded like styrene plastic, so CA glue could be used. However, there is still the chance that the glue joints could eventually fail. In building Korber's Aunt Millie's House and Railroad Avenue's Blue Bird Cafe, I used a silicone method similar to the one described above, but with one difference. Cast-resin buildings are made with thinner wall sections that must be joined using butt joints. In other words, one edge of the wall is glued to the next, as opposed to having a positive mechanical joint.

I use CA to glue the walls together (as per the manufacturer's instructions). However, I do not depend on CA for a permanent bond, but rather to just hold the joint in place temporarily. I then apply a bead of silicone along each inside edge and add a square strip of wood to the corners for reinforcement. A strip ¼" x ¼" or ½" x ½" cut to the length of the joint works fine. This wood provides additional gluing surface for the joint. Press these strips into the

This cast-resin structure's joints have been reinforced with clear silicone and pieces of stripwood. Wood gives the silicone more surface area to adhere to, while the silicone strengthens the joints. The structure was initially assembled with CA, which held the walls and roof temporarily in place.

Resin was used to reinforce the joints of this resin structure. The thickening agent Cab-O-Sil was added to prevent the resin from running off while being applied.

inside corners and coat them on all sides with the silicone that was applied to the joint earlier. This method makes the structure very strong. You'll have difficulty getting one apart after the silicone cures.

Epoxy is another means of gluing cast-resin structures together. This two-part glue is very strong, but is slower curing and will require clamping while it cures. (See chapter 2.)

The best method I have found for reinforcing resin structures is "resin reinforcing." Here's how it works. Before assembling, rough up the inside edges with sandpaper from about ½" back from the edge. Assemble the structure using CA as above. Seal each seam by applying masking tape to all of the outside corners of the structure. Mix a

3 Another example on Dart and Dot Rinefort's railroad is the Rinefort Bros. Mercantile, which was kitbashed form two Piko kits.

A look at the interior reveals how the kits were merged. The extra wall from one of the kits was used to fill the void between the two peaked roofs to produce a new wall. Likewise, the roof sections (left) were combined to make one larger roof.

batch of casting resin and add a thickening agent called Cab-O-Sil. Experiment with the ratios—I use about one tablespoon per two ounces. This product will change the uncured resin into a thicker material that can be poured and worked into the corners of the structure. Apply this mixture to all joints. (You may have to do this in steps.) When cured, the joints will be quite solid.

Painting

A coat of paint is always a good idea, even on pre-painted buildings. It protects the plastic from the sun's harmful ultraviolet rays. Paint is a must on uncolored cast-resin buildings for both looks and protection. I have used a variety of paints on plastic, including acrylic paints, spray enamels, or my favorite, Floquil model railroad paint. If you are a serious modeler, an airbrush is another must. It will enable you to achieve a smooth and professional paint job.

I have found that most paints work

This transfer depot/freight office from Garden-Texture (No. 31599) is an example of a commercial kit featuring wood (redwood and cedar) construction.

best if applied over a good primer. I use a spray can primer such as Krylon. Model paints applied over primer also hold up well outdoors. I recently removed one of my original Pola buildings from the railroad. It had been painted and placed outdoors in May 1988, and removed in February 1994. The original paint, though faded, was still intact. See chapter 13 for more on painting.

Repair and maintenance

The only maintenance required on carefully constructed and painted plastic buildings may be an occasional repainting of the roof. For small repairs, such as replacing broken detail pieces, I have found that E-6000 and Quick Grab work well (see chapter 2). They both are weatherproof and strong. I have found that solvent glues are not very effective on weathered plastic.

Occasionally, a plastic building will warp. (You may even find a warped piece in a brand-new kit.) This usually can be fixed. In the case of small cast-resin parts, you can use a hair dryer to warm and soften the part. It can then be worked back into shape and cooled.

For larger cast-resin parts, such as walls and roofs, and styrene parts like Pola building components, higher heat may be in order. Hot water can be used for these parts. We have a hot-water dispenser on our kitchen sink that works well for this. If you don't have one of these, you can also use boiling water. Warm up the parts in the water and work them back into shape.

On rare occasion, a brace may be required to prevent the part from warping again. Braces can be made of plywood, wooden battens, or other similar materials. Glue the brace to the backside of the part. A brace may have to be screwed or nailed in place.

Bases

Placing your buildings on bases serves several purposes. A base provides a solid platform upon which a structure can rest. It also keeps a building out of the dirt. See Chapter 14 for more on bases.

Kitbashing

Kitbashing is a way to customize a commercial kit. Simple kitbashing could include such changes as cutting down the size of the building, adding dormer windows or extra doors, removing doors, combining two structures to make one, or changing the roofline or roofing material. Modifications are limited only by your imagination.

Many garden railway societies have swap meets where you can find second-hand buildings. These are good (and inexpensive) for potential kitbashing.

Wooden kits

It's worth mentioning that wooden structure kits are available in large scale. Houseworks Ltd. (http://www.houseworksltd.com/) is a supplier of a variety of miniature wooden dollhouse parts in both 1:24 and 1:12 scale.

Smith Pond Junction Railroad Products and Garden-Texture both offer numerous products for the garden railroader, including a wide variety of wooden kits and accessories. I will cover wood construction in chapter 6.

SOURCES

Cab-o-sil
www.eagerplastics.com/cab.htm

Evergreen Scale Models
18620-F 141 Ave. NE
Woodinville, WA 98072
www.evergreenscalemodels.com

Garden-Texture
P.O. Box 4111
Canton, GA 30114
gardentexture.com

Muella Scale Models
1161 Hinestown Rd.
Jacksonville, NC 28540
muellascalemodels.com

Piko
Distributed by Silvergate Distributors Inc.
9755 Birch Canyon Place, Ste. 200
San Diego, CA 92126
www.silvergatedistributors.com

Pola
Distributed by Wm. K. Walthers, Inc.
800-487-2467
www.walthers.com

Smith Pond Railroad Junction
www.spjrr.net

The author built this plank-on-frame sawmill for Charlie and Pam Allen. The challenge was to fit a large facility like this in the area available. The complex had to be compressed yet still maintain the character of the original inspirational prototype.

CHAPTER 4

Scratchbuilding

Learning how to scratchbuild structures will open up a whole new world for you. While kits have much to offer, there may come a time when you want to build something special. You may wish to re-create a structure from your childhood, like an old schoolhouse, a summer home, or a family store, or you may want to add an industry for your railroad to serve. A scratchbuilt structure personalizes your garden railway.

▶ The Coldwater Canyon Sawmill is loosely based on the second sawmill of the Sanger Lumber company in the Converse Basin of California. I used selective compression to fit the mill into the allocated space. If I had built in full-scale size, this structure would have taken up half of the layout. My goal was to capture the flavor of a large mill even though it was in a small space. This structure is completely scratchbuilt, including the windows. It is plank-on-frame construction. Planks are nailed and the battens are glued with Titebond III waterproof wood glue. The roof is wood sheathed and covered, with wet-dry sandpaper cut into strips to simulate roofing paper. The wood was left untreated so it would weather naturally.

In choosing what to build, keep a few things in mind. What is the purpose of the structure? Just as in designing your railroad, you have a specific theme in mind when designing and ultimately placing your model structures. What do you want the structure to represent? A section house can be placed along the right-of-way where there are no other buildings to suggest an isolated area. Other structures, such as cabins, can indicate a temporary settlement or a place that is used seasonally. On the other hand, a formal building like a bank, train depot, or school would indicate it is part of a permanent settlement.

Most garden railroads have a limited amount of space for buildings, so you should give some thought to how to use your space. On my railroad, I have designated "no-build" spaces, and other spaces for towns. I also have a few outpost and temporary settlements.

I like to find my subjects in the full-size world whenever possible. Modeling structures from reality will give your railroad a unique look, and research is half the fun of model building. Working within a specific theme or time period offers the challenges of learning about a certain era and its surrounding history. You become a historian of sorts. I take my camera along on my travels so I can photograph interesting buildings. If you are modeling contemporary structures, a trip into town or out into the country with a camera is all that's required.

Some of the nicest compliments I receive about my railroad are when people tell me my town reminds them of some place they have been. My towns are not models of specific places, but I model full-size buildings, so it gives the town the feel of authenticity.

Other sources of subjects are books and magazines. I have collected a large number of books on Victorian houses, ghost towns, local history, and styles of architecture. These have been a great source of information and inspiration.

One of my richest resources has been *Narrow Gauge & Short Line Gazette*. This magazine features photos and plans for the types of structures I like to build. *Up Clear Creek on the Narrow Gauge*, by Harry W. Brunk, is a compilation of several articles that he wrote for the *Gazette*. I have used the plans in this book to build several structures.

Though I prefer to build structures from the real world, you could use model kits or photos of existing models as a basis for large-scale scratchbuilt structures. Sometimes an HO or N scale kit is inexpensive enough to buy just for the plans.

Plans

Whenever possible, I like to build models to scale, though this is not my main concern. I try to build things in proportion so that they look good together. I consider myself a "scene builder." I include enough detail to make my structures believable. I happen

These plans are based on a small house I photographed in Colorado. I drew it to full size and made a mock-up directly from the plans. To compress it, I kept the doors and windows the same but reduced all the other dimensions by 10 percent. The cut-out figures represent three popular garden railway scales (left to right): 1:20.3, 1:22.5, and 1:24. All three scales could be used, even though the building is technically 1:24 scale. See the actual model using these plans in chapter 6 on advanced wood construction.

Conversion Chart

The following is a quick reference for changing scales. To convert from one scale to another, look up the scale you are at across the top and read down until the row is the scale you want. This is your multiplier. For example, to convert measurements taken from an S scale drawing to N scale, look across the top row for S and down to the N row to get 0.400. Multiply the S dimension by 0.4 to get the N scale measure.

	current scale								
desired scale	F (1:20.3)	G (1:22.5)	#1 (1:32)	O (1:48)	S (1:64)	HO (1:87.1)	TT (1:120)	N (1:160)	Z (1:220)
F	1.000	1.108	1.576	2.365	3.153	4.291	5.911	7.882	10.837
G	0.902	1.000	1.422	2.133	2.844	3.871	5.333	7.111	9.778
#1	0.634	0.703	1.000	1.500	2.000	2.722	3.750	5.000	6.875
O	0.423	0.469	0.667	1.000	1.333	1.815	2.500	3.333	4.583
S	0.317	0.352	0.500	0.750	1.000	1.361	1.875	2.500	3.438
HO	0.233	0.258	0.367	0.551	0.735	1.000	1.378	1.837	2.526
TT	0.169	0.188	0.267	0.400	0.533	0.726	1.000	1.333	1.833
N	0.127	0.141	0.200	0.300	0.400	0.544	0.750	1.000	1.375
Z	0.092	0.102	0.145	0.218	0.291	0.396	0.545	0.727	1.000

Selective compression

This picture of the Star Hook & Ladder Company in Georgetown, Colo., illustrates how selective compression works. The late Pam Allen wanted a firehouse that would fit into the town on her Coldwater Canyon Railroad. We looked through several books and found this nice little firehouse. We found several photos taken in different years; some photos showed the building with a balcony, some with a roof overhang, and in some the doors and windows had been added or removed. The belfry was in different states of repair. These photos reminded us that buildings change during their lifetimes, so don't worry about being too exact. We want to capture the essence of the structure, not necessarily make an exact copy.

For the Allens' line, we decided on a version with the balcony. You can tell from the photo that the model has been compressed; it's two-thirds as deep as the actual building. The spacing between the doors and the edge of the walls is more compressed on the model, and the same is true with the upper-story windows. Pam wanted to be able to park her 1912 Christy front pumper in the firehouse, so we raised the main doors to accommodate the engine's tall smokestack. Such modifications were common practice on real buildings when new pieces of equipment were obtained.

Next to the fire-engine doors, we left out a window to accommodate the new, larger doors. We discovered this had actually been done to the prototype building when we found some original photos. This coincidence reinforces the point about buildings changing over time.

Even though many things are different from the original, what is important are the details that make the model building resemble its prototype. The roofline at the peak is a unique feature of the original structure, as is the relative placement of doors. The corner trim, the belfry, and the fire-station insignia above the windows all contribute to the character of the building. By re-creating these details you can make a credible replica without having to build an exact scale model. Most observers would not even notice the differences; it's the similarities they will see.

to work in 1:24 (½"=1'), so I'll be using this particular scale in my discussion. If you are building in 1:22.5, 1:20.3, or 1:32, you will have to convert dimensions to your desired scale. When I refer to "large scale," I am including all the above scales. The basic construction methods are the same. You can find a scale conversion chart at www.urbaneagle.com/data/RRconvcharts.html

Even a small building in the full-size world can become quite big in large scale. This is something to consider if, like most of us, you are working with limited space.

Selective compression

To economize on space and build a believable structure, you can use a technique called "selective compression." Certain dimensions are cut down to make the model smaller yet still retain its character and credible proportions. Some HO kits have been compressed in this manner. In HO scale, space is at a premium even more so than in the garden.

This is another structure spotted in Silverton, Colo. Its original use is unclear but it looks like a small barn, carriage house, or garage. This building was selected as a subject because it is small and has many interesting elements, such as wood siding, a metal roof on one side, and tarpaper on the other. It will make an interesting little model. A building like this could also be used as a speeder shed or as a maintenance-of-way structure.

Here is a 1/32 scale model of the Lackawanna Terminal in Hoboken, N.J. A courtyard sits in front of the station, with the Ferry House on the left. The waiting area at right has been greatly compressed to fit the available space.

A modern photo of the prototype Ferry House on which the 1952 model was based. The model was selectively compressed to get everything to fit into the available space.

When compressing a structure, make the ground-floor doors and windows to the correct scale. An average doorway is around seven feet tall (this scales to 3.5" in 1:24). A quick way to check to see if a door is the proper size is to place a scale figure next to it.

Once doors and windows are correctly scaled, you can start compressing. (Windows can actually be made slightly smaller than scale.) If the side wall of a structure is 30 feet long (15" in 1:24 scale), for example, you could reduce it to 24 feet (12") without losing the flavor of the building.

After you have decided on a building to model, a plan of it on paper will be a great help.

If the building you are contemplating is small enough, a full-size drawing is a good idea. This will allow you to see the actual size of the structure in advance.

In most cases, the most important feature of the structure is its facade. If, when planning a facade, you put the windows and doors in their correct relative positions, you can cut down the overall width of the building by trimming the wall areas, including spaces between doors and windows. The second story can also be compressed. The next time you are at Disneyland, look at the Main Street buildings. You will notice that the second stories are compressed to give the illusion of taller buildings. The second story is not full height and the openings are smaller.

For many years I drew full-size plans on old manila folders. They open up to 12" x 18" and, being made of thick paper, are durable. (Durability is important when working with plans in a workshop.) Manila-folder plans can also be used as templates for cutting out window and door openings. A template is handy if you plan to make more than one of an item, such as identical right- and left-hand walls. You can even make mock-ups using the manila folders.

Today I use my computer to make drawings, using Corel Draw software. The main reason for this is that I have been using a laser cutter to make many of my parts. To use any computer-numeric-controlled (CNC) machine, you need a vector drawing. Since I have to make a drawing for these parts, I found it just as easy to make a complete drawing for the structure. If you are computer literate, learning this program should not be difficult.

A simple, smaller-scale drawing on a piece of graph paper will also work. In fact, it is a must if the structure you plan to build is very large. I use graph paper divided into a ¼" grid, and I make my drawings to a scale of ¼" (or one grid box) = 1" of the model (a quarter-size drawing of the model). It is much easier to make changes on paper than on the work itself.

SOURCES

Narrow Gauge & Short Line Gazette
P.O. Box 26
Los Altos, CA 94023
www.ngslgazette.com
800-545-4102

Basic wood construction

CHAPTER 5

In real life, wood structures are made by assembling a framework of lumber, covering it with sheathing, and applying protective siding material over the sheathing. About the simplest method of duplicating these structures for a garden railway is to build a solid building shell and apply siding over it. This can be done to represent many types of buildings.

Wood structures, like this two-stall engine house, can be built by gluing strips over a solid-wall shell to represent board-and-batten siding.

Crystal Springs Station is an example of a structure built using the plank-on-solid-wall method of construction.

LESSONS LEARNED FROM THE CRYSTAL SPRINGS STATION PROJECT:
- Wooden dollhouse trim does not hold up outdoors.
- Plywood will hold up well if it is fully protected, in this case by external planking.
- Structures should be kept off the ground by using a base.
- Silicone works very well in holding wood parts together (especially to hold roof shingles in place).

Crystal Springs Station

When I built my first Crystal Springs Station in 1990, I wanted an unfinished, wood-planked building that would weather naturally. The method I used to do this was plank-on-solid.

For this structure, I built a full shell out of ½"-thick plywood and cut out spaces for doors and windows. Next, I cut scale redwood planks from larger stock with a table saw. I applied and glued the planks, even over door and window openings, with Titebond III. Completely cover the plywood shell with planks. I let the glue dry, then nailed the planks with brads from a brad gun. I cut out door and window openings with a Dremel tool with a router bit, cutting through the planks that covered the window openings.

I made wood window frames so they would match rest of the structure and weather naturally. To allow the glazing to fit in behind the frame, I overlapped the window cutouts. I made glazing pieces out of clear acrylic sheet, cut to size, and glued them in place with clear silicone. After the silicone cured, I made the window mullions out of wood and glued them directly to the glazing with silicone.

Dollhouse details formed the trim work for Crystal Springs Station, including an interesting Victorian ridge cap that I found at a shop. The cap was made from two pieces of wood and, after a short time outdoors, the decorative part came loose from the base. The original glue was obviously not weatherproof, so I simply let the weather take its course. When the scalloped section came off completely, I glued it back in place with silicone. I've had no problem with the cap since then.

I added scratchbuilt Gothic trim to this structure. I made lightning rods from dollhouse furniture legs, beads, and small finishing nails. The chimney is two Houseworks brick corner-pieces glued together to form a square tube. Finally, I added an extra course of bricks cut from a piece of plastic stock.

The station was durable and would probably have been around for a long time. It had shown little deterioration over years. Unfortunately, this building was destroyed in 1996 when a large pine tree fell into our yard.

Parts have been cut out to match the plans shown on page 35. Edges are best cut using a table saw, but you can use a band saw or even a hand saw. Masonite is easy to work with. The door and window openings were cut out using a scroll saw; a router or zip cutter would also work. In the upper left-hand corner is roofing material—180-grit wet/dry sandpaper. This can be cut with scissors or a hobby knife. Warning: The sandpaper will ruin a good pair of scissors, so use an old pair.

Use a square to mark the lines where the battens will be placed.

The structure was designed so the right and left walls fit over the ends of the front and rear walls. I first glued the braces to the edges of the front and rear walls.

My table saw does not tilt, so I used my belt sander to bevel the top edge of the roof sections.

Board-and-batten

Board-and-batten, a popular method of construction for many years, is relatively easy to duplicate in miniature. Start with a solid shell. You can build the shell from a thinner material, such as Masonite, since battens will not be nailed on in this process. For more on Masonite, see the materials chapter.

I made a plan for a small structure (see page 35): a shed with a simple peaked roof and board-and-batten siding. I chose this because it is an easy style to duplicate. I built this project in 1:24 scale.

Using my plans, I cut out the walls and roof with a table saw. Then, using a scroll saw, I cut out spaces for the doors and windows. For this project, I am using commercially-produced windows and doors (Grandt Line No. 3930 windows and a No. 3936 door). These doors and windows have a trim piece around them. If you are a little off with your measurements, the frame will hide any imperfections.

Once you have made the walls and roof parts, assemble the basic structure. To ensure a strong bond, I use wooden stakes as corner braces, which increases the gluing surface. I use nominal ½"-square redwood, glued in place with Titebond III.

I am using wood battens for this project, but you may also use plastic (more on this in chapter 8). I cut battens using a table saw. Full-size battens can vary in width, averaging about 3" or 4" wide and about 1" thick. A strip

The walls are assembled with support blocks in the corners. I installed blocks on the upper interior surfaces of the right and left wall to support the roof and to increase the gluing surface.

Wood reinforcing pieces have been installed along every interior joint, adding strength and providing additional gluing surface.

The battens have been added. Make a frame around the window and door openings so the frames fit up against the windows and doors.

The building has been painted inside and out with a heavy-duty primer. Latex house paint provides long-lasting protection against the elements. After you apply a good base coat, finish the building with the color of your choice. Model paints hold up fairly well with a good primer under them. The building is now ready for the finishing touches.

SOURCE
Grandt Line Products
1040 B Shary Ct.
Concord, CA 94518
www.grandtline.com

⅛" to 3⁄16" wide and 1⁄16" thick will work nicely for ½" scale battens. You can also buy ready-cut scale model lumber at a hobby shop.

Batten spacing varies. I am using a scale foot, but they can be closer if you prefer. Use a T-square and a pencil to mark where the battens will be applied, and glue them in place with Titebond III. Note: Use batten material to frame in the window and door openings. This will allow for proper installation of the doors and windows.

Paint the entire building inside and out. Use a good-quality exterior paint, such as latex house paint. Don't worry about color—this is just a base coat for protection. When detailing the building, you can use model paints to achieve the colors you want. Note: If you are using thick house paint you may see brush marks. Take advantage of this by brushing vertically so the brush marks look like wood grain.

Paint doors and windows before installation. After I paint the finish coat on the walls, I then secure the windows and doors with a touch of silicone. Note: silicone does not bond well with styrene. The silicone is just to make the window fit snugly and to allow for future removal, if necessary. If your doors and windows fit tightly enough on their own, you don't need to use silicone.

These windows and doors are plastic so they will last almost forever. If your Masonite building disintegrates in 20 years, you can still reuse the windows and doors.

Tool shed templates

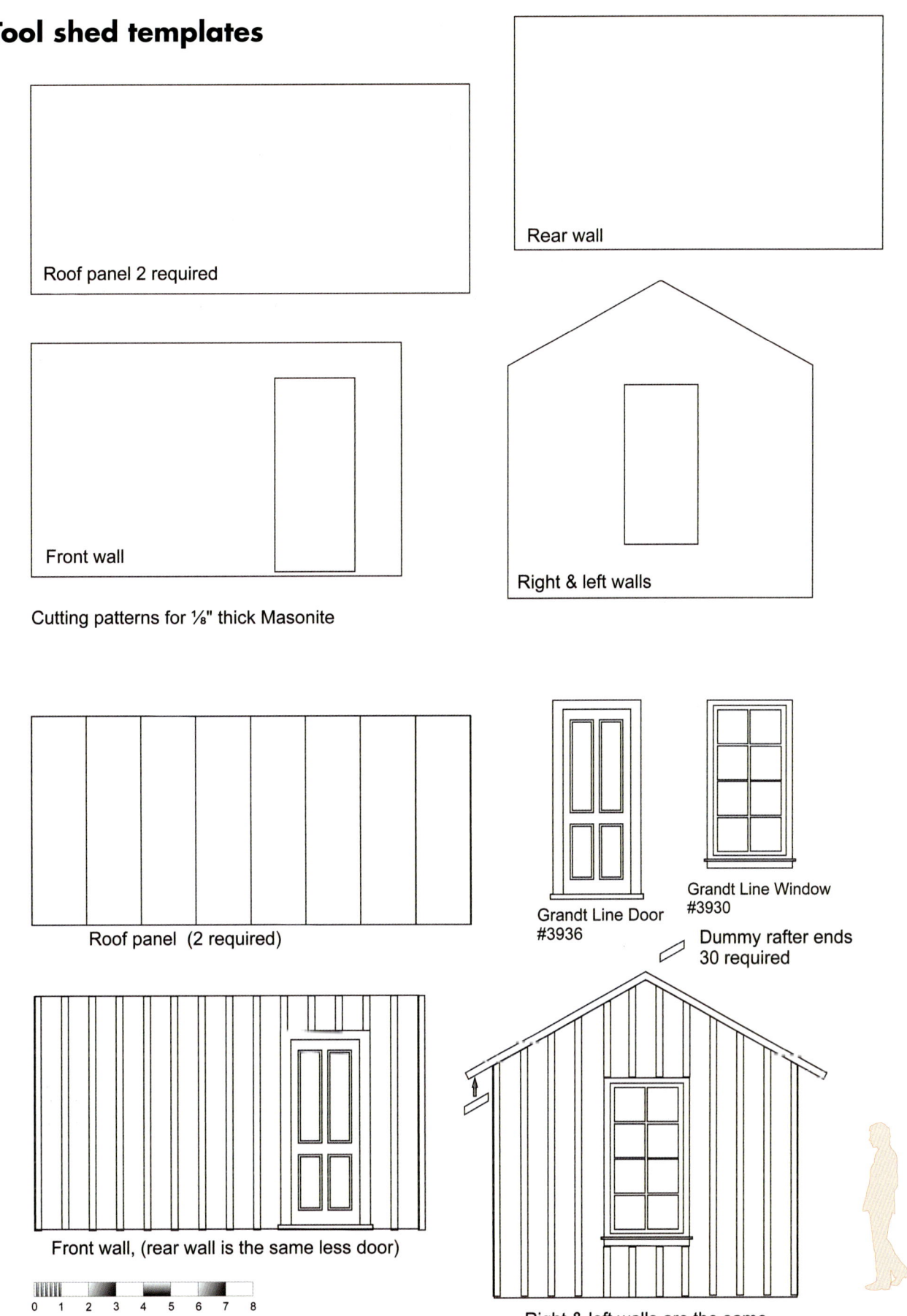

Cutting patterns for ⅛" thick Masonite

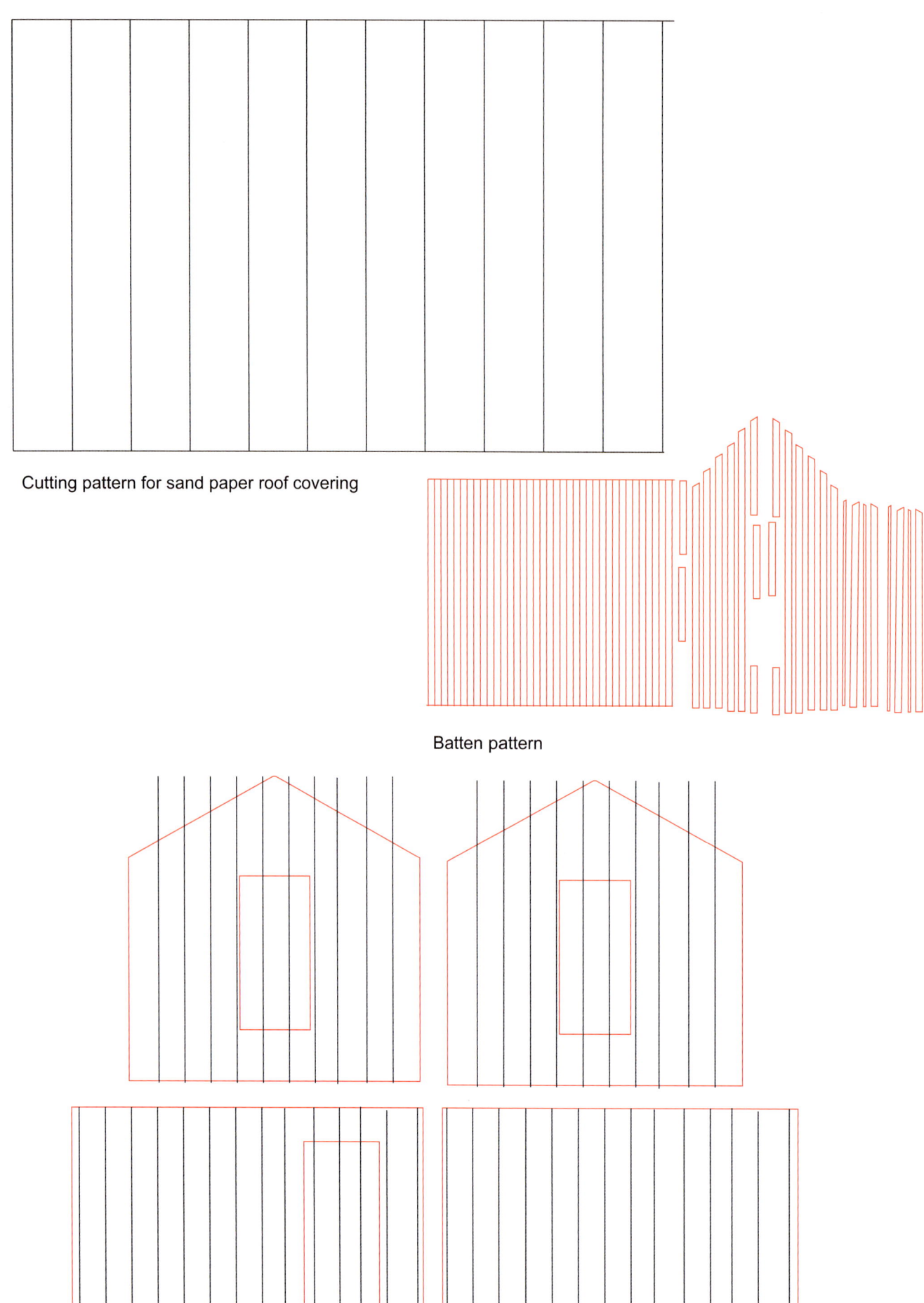

Cutting pattern for sand paper roof covering

Batten pattern

Batten positions

Advanced wood construction

CHAPTER 6

There is nothing like real wood. It is fun to work with and it looks good. I highly recommend the use of a pin nailer to make building scale wooden structures for your outdoor railroad much easier. A pin nailer allows you to nail small pieces in place, which in turn means you can use finely cut lumber to create a more realistic building.

Using real wood helps garden railway structures capture the look of real weathered wood structures, such as the store in the inset photo.

Drawings are placed in clear plastic page protectors. The plans can be used as a template to cut timbers to correct size. The timbers are glued and nailed with the pin nailer.

Here's the assembled timber structure.

Now it's sided with boards ready for battens.

The nice thing about this method is you will have details on the inside as well as outside.

Plank-on-frame construction

For this project, I've selected a small wooden outbuilding in Silverton, Colo., as my inspiration (see page 39). It looks like it was originally a small barn or carriage house with an annex.

First, build a frame. I use a framing system similar to the method in which old barns where made. It is a simple frame built up from 6"-square beams.

Mill the lumber using a table saw. See chapter 3 for details on milling wood. Next, cut the timbers to length as per the plans. Nail the framing together. Since a pin nailer's pins do not have heads, they will not hold by themselves, and you must apply a little glue to the wood. I use a drop of Titebond III. The pin will hold the timbers together while the glue dries.

After the frame is assembled and has time to dry, pin and glue the boards and battens in place. To add strength to the pins, insert them at an angle, and alternate the angle as you pin each plank. This will help bind the planks in place.

The walls can be pre-assembled, or you can build the frame as you would do with a full-size building. In either case, add 6" x 6" corner pieces where the interior walls come together. Roof rafters can be built the same way as the wall framing. Once the rafters are complete, pin and glue the roof battens in place.

Select your roofing material. The full-size building has areas of wood shingles, tar paper, and corrugated metal. It may have had three or four different types of roofs over its lifespan, so you have options of what type of roof you'd like to add.

If you choose to build a structure that is not board-on-batten but something like clapboard or novelty siding, you need a frame with more vertical studs. Modern buildings use a standard stud spacing of 16", but older structures often had 24" spacing between studs.

For this type of frame, you can make a generic framing jig with wooden blocks as guides. The blocks will space the studs at a scale 16" or 24" spacing.

Pin nailer

A 23-gauge pin nailer is a great tool to have. In fact, it is a must-have if you plan to build structures out of scale lumber. These pins have no heads, so they should be reinforced with glue. A trick to a better nail grip is to nail at an angle and reverse the angle at every other point. Note: Even though the pins do not have a head, they do have a point on one end. Pay attention to the arrow on the strip of pins. Make sure it points down toward the work when loading the gun.

The battens have been added above the joints between the planks.

This view shows the crosspieces that will hold the roof.

Lay the studs in place in the jig. Assemble the frame by gluing and pinning the upper and lower plates to the studs.

Start installing the planks. Use a drop of Titebond II, then pin the plank to the studs. Remember, the pins in a pin nailer have limited holding power. Angling the nailer about 20 degrees one way and then 20 degrees the opposite way as you add pins to form a stronger attachment.

I call this a "generic" framing jig because there is no provision for doors or windows. You will have to decide where these openings will be located, then add appropriate headers and rough sills. To do this, pin up your frame, leaving out the studs where the windows and doors will be located. You can then remove the frame from the jig and add the headers and sills.

This same method can be used to build any plank-and-frame structure. In some cases, you may be using scale 12" beams. In this case, you can use an 18-gauge brad since this size of lumber is less likely to split when being nailed.

I fit this structure with an ABS plastic roof. You'll find more detailed information on this process in chapter 8.

This is my roundhouse as it was being built. It is a plank-on-frame structure and constructed in the same manner as a full-size building. Construction started with a frame, followed by planks nailed in place. The roof is wood sheathing with wet/dry sandpaper strips held in place with silicone. The structure is painted with a coat of red primer.

Wooden outbuilding templates

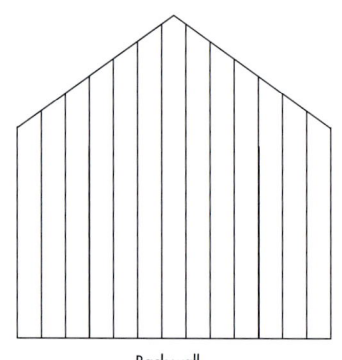

Back wall

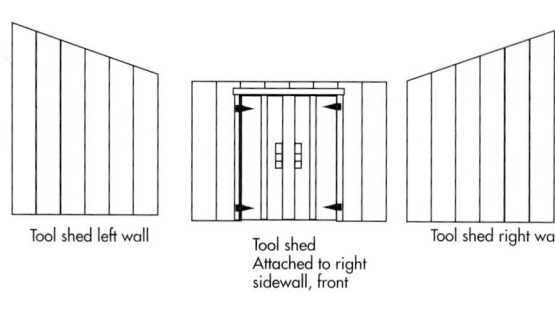

Tool shed left wall   Tool shed Attached to right sidewall, front   Tool shed right wall

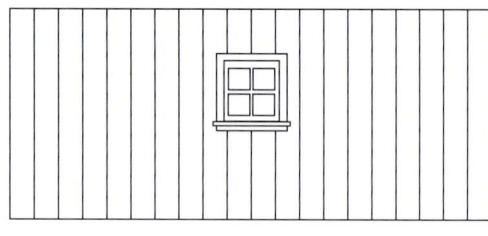

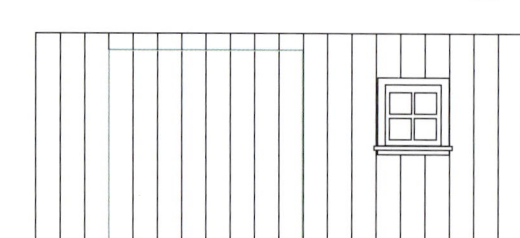

Left side wall

Tool shed location   Right side wall

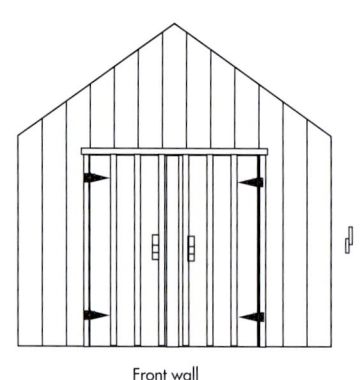

Front wall

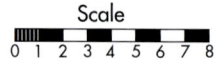

Scale
0 1 2 3 4 5 6 7 8

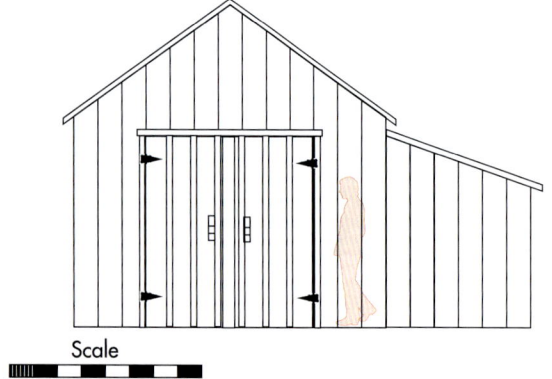

Scale
0 1 2 3 4 5 6 7 8

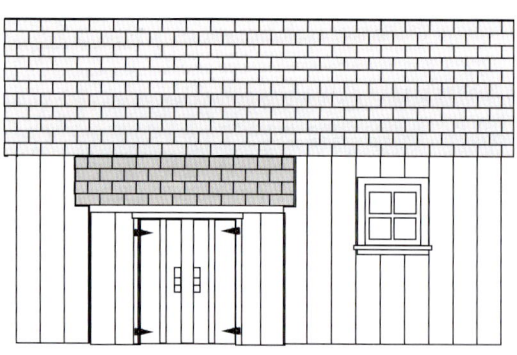

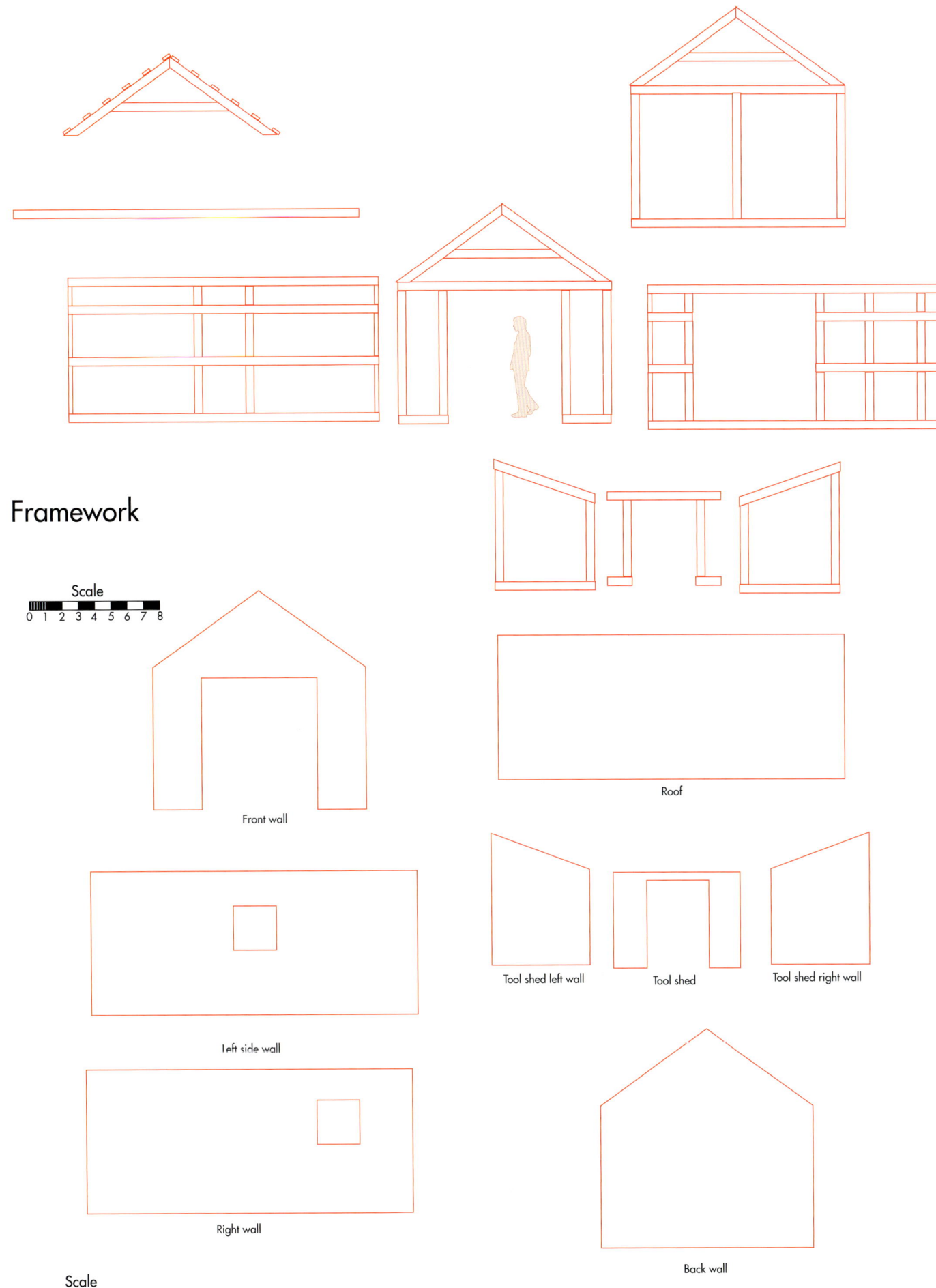

A solid wall is cut out, then redwood strips are glued to the wall.

The wall is completely planked over.

Table saw with zero clearance

Cutting scale lumber can be dangerous with the wrong equipment. You must have a zero clearance table so small pieces of lumber do not fall down into the blade hole or, worse yet, kick back. This table can be made by using a piece of plywood or Masonite. On most table saws, you can use your existing fence. Set it so it is exactly parallel to the saw's blade. Lower the blade, then place a piece of Masonite on the table flush to the fence. Secure it with clamps, then turn on the saw and run the blade up through the Masonite. You will now have a zero clearance table.

In the top photo, I used a piece of maple as a fence. This method is also useful on other of saws such as bandsaws that may not have a fence. They can be rigged like this for cutting planks. If you use a band saw, select a wide blade for cutting planks. You can make or buy a set of simple gauges (right). These will help you align your fence and set the size you need. Each gauge represents a different board width.

Window and door openings are cut out using the solid wall as a guide. This should be done only after the glue has thoroughly dried.

Plank-on-solid construction

This method is similar to the method used in chapter 5 using Masonite and wood battens.

I'm making a model based on a small Colorado row house. Instead of a frame, I cut walls from Masonite. Next, I cut planks from wood using the methods discussed earlier. Before assembling the walls, I cover the Masonite with the wood planks, using Titebond III. So the walls would fit together neatly later, I left a slight overhang of planks. It is easier to cut out the doors and windows with a scroll saw than it is to cut them later with a jig saw. Once the planks are glued in place and allowed to dry, cut out the door and window openings.

Glue the walls together with Titebond I. In each interior corner, I added a ½"-square reinforcing piece. Pin and glue the corner moldings and wood trim pieces in place. I used a sheet of Masonite as a sub-roof and engraved ABS plastic as the final roof material.

I used Grandt Line windows, doors, and trim. They are made of styrene and painted primer gray, with a final coat of green acrylic paint.

My intention is to let this building weather naturally. Since I used redwood, I started the weathering process by brushing on some baking soda and water (two tablespoons baking soda to one cup of water). Brush the solution onto the wood and let it dry.

These are the basic walls that will form the shell of the building. You could assemble solid walls like these first and then plank them.

I prefer to plank walls before assembly because that makes it easier to cut the window and door openings. Notice the slight overlap of the planking. This allows for a more-solid corner joint once the walls are assembled.

Walls are assembled using the same method shown in chapter 5 with bracing strips in the corners.

A Masonite roof is added.

Corner trim and trim along the roofline are secured with glue and a pin nailer.

I want this building to weather naturally so I have not painted or treated the wood. To speed the weathering process, I mixed a tablespoon of baking soda in a cup of water and applied the mixture to the redwood. This causes the wood to turn gray.

Row house templates

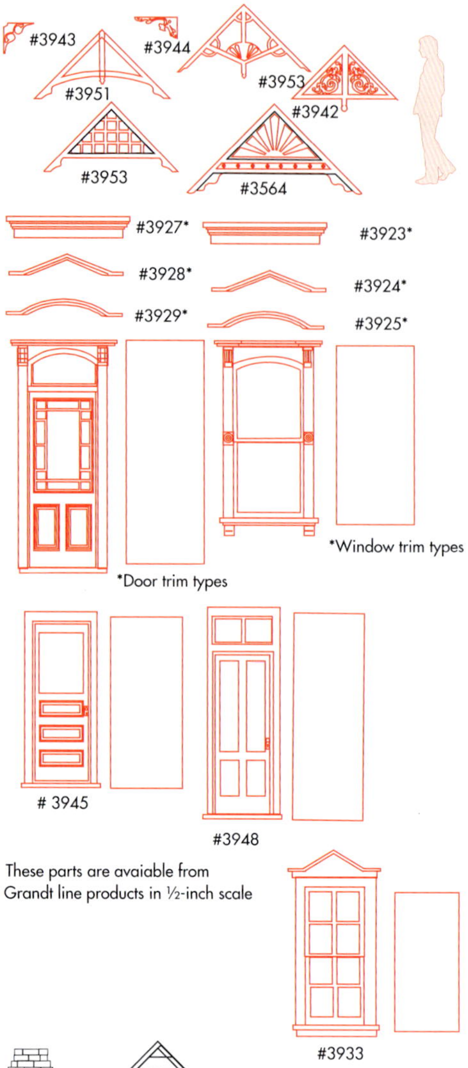

#3943
#3944
#3951
#3953
#3942
#3953
#3564
#3927*
#3923*
#3928*
#3924*
#3929*
#3925*

*Door trim types

*Window trim types

#3945
#3948

These parts are avaiable from Grandt line products in ½-inch scale

#3933

Scale
0 1 2 3 4 5 6 7 8

44

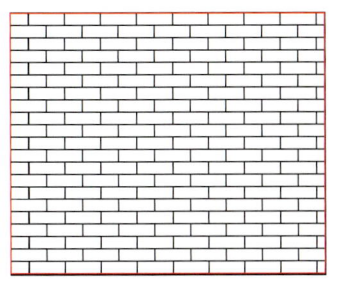
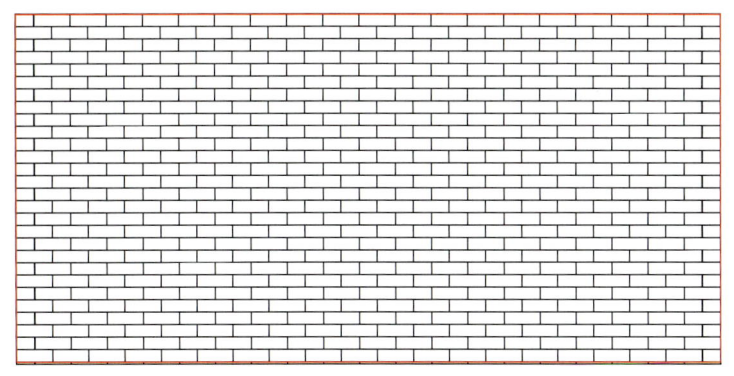

Two required

Roof templates

Scale
0 1 2 3 4 5 6 7 8

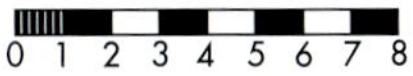

CHAPTER 7

This photo shows a good example of how only three structures can suggest an entire business district.

Doors, windows, and trim

Every structure has at least one door and, in most cases, one or more windows. Doors and windows help give a structure its personality. A Victorian house, for example, has highly ornate windows, whereas the windows of a miner's shack are likely to be crude.

A large number of plastic windows and doors are available commercially from hobby shops or mail-order suppliers. Grandt Line Products, in particular, has a large selection.

The company's windows are clean and crisp, and include plastic glazing. Commercial windows are a good choice for beginners, because making your own windows can be time consuming.

Still, it is good to know how to make windows in case you want to create a structure with a unique style of windows and doors. The most basic method works well for structures that are seen from a distance.

A wide variety of cast windows is available from Grandt Line.

Simple windows

To make a simple window, cut an opening in the wall and make a window casing or frame around it. The casing can be as simple as a plain wooden border or as elaborate as a Victorian window adorned with gingerbread. At this point, you have a window without glass or mullions.

Cut a piece of clear acrylic slightly larger than the window opening. A margin of ¼" to ½" all around is adequate. For most types of windows, use clear acrylic, but for a special effect you could use tinted or non-glare acrylic, which is slightly translucent. If you are comfortable working with glass, you may substitute it for plastic in your windows.

Apply automobile pinstriping tape to the acrylic, horizontally and vertically as desired, to simulate mullions. Attach a tape border to form a frame around the mullions. Apply silicone to the edges of the acrylic, then insert the window to the interior window opening (**fig. 1**).

I chose wood in this application because it is easy to work with. Be aware that wood has a limited lifespan outdoors. Don't use woods like basswood. Choose wood that weathers better, such as redwood or cedar.

Simple doors

Make a door using a similar method as the window. Cut a door opening into the wall and frame it. If you want a glass door, apply clear acrylic and pinstripe tape as described above. To simulate a wood-paneled door, use any

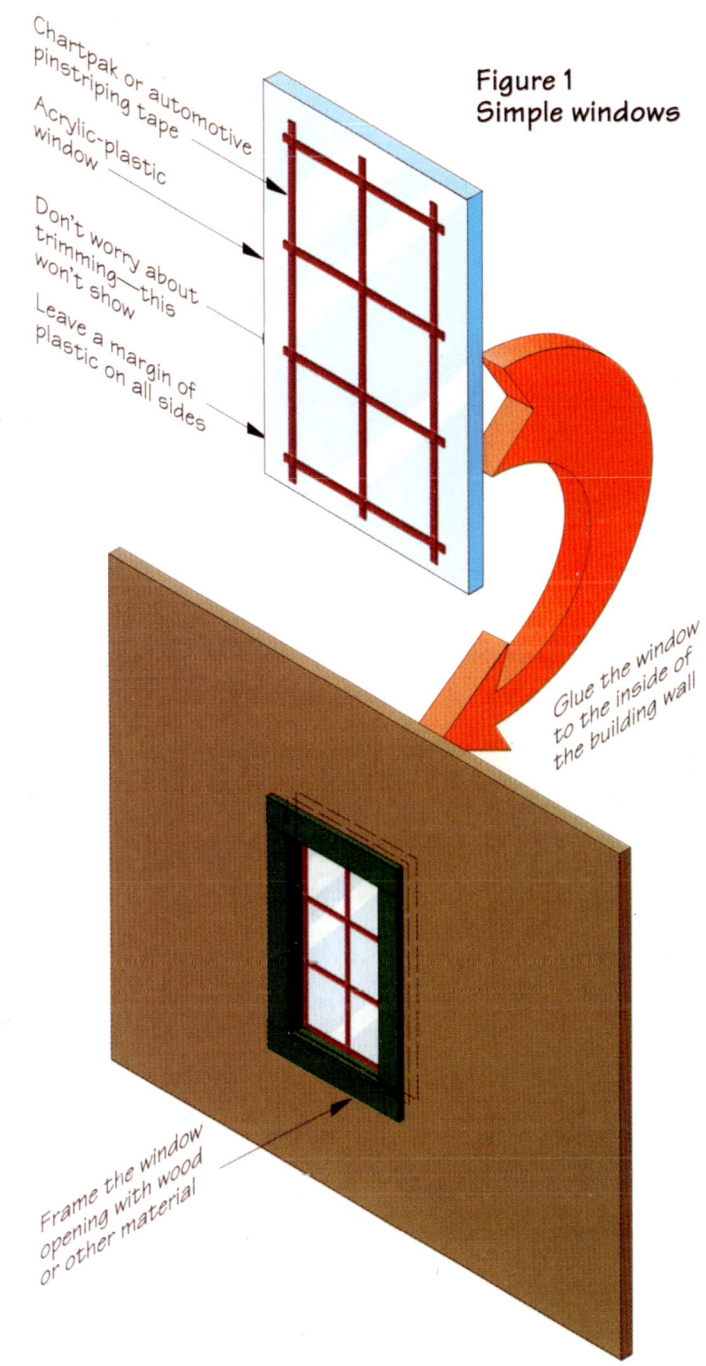

Figure 2
Simple doors

relatively smooth material, such as Masonite. Cut wide automotive pinstriping tape (or electrical tape) to the desired width to frame the door panels. Apply the tape in the same way you did for the windows. Leave a margin in the door material around the outside edge of the door. Glue the door in place with silicone from the interior wall (**fig. 2**).

Close-up windows and doors

This method is better for windows and doors that can be closely observed. Make a window or door opening as described above. Cut out a piece of acrylic as before. Using wood strips, make a window frame that will snugly fit within the window opening. Attach the wood frame directly to the acrylic, using Killer Red adhesive or 3M's 4011 or 4010 mounting tape, described in chapter 2. When finished, you will have a window with three-dimensional mullions. Glue the window in on the interior side of the structure.

If you want a natural wood look, do not paint the mullions. However, if you desire painted mullions, paint them prior to gluing (**fig. 3**).

Similarly, you can make a door using this method. Cut a basic door panel and attach wood veneer or thin wooden planks using Quick Grip, epoxy, or Titebond III. To prevent warping, place a weight, such as a heavy book, over the door while it dries. (see figure 3).

If you need to make several windows or doors, use a jig to ensure their sizes are kept constant. A simple jig can be made by cutting an opening exactly the same size as your window opening in a small piece of wood. Line up window frames and mullions in the jig for an accurate fit.

In chapter 8, I will discuss making windows out of plastic.

Shades and blinds

Plain windows and doors can be boring, but with a little imagination, you can dress them up to bring your buildings to life.

If your building has no interior, you may want to disguise that fact. You want to create the illusion that your structure is more than an empty box. Fog or frost the windows by spraying the glazing with Testor's Dullcote or a similar product. You can also sand the glazing lightly with 400-grit sandpaper. Fogged windows allow light to pass and suggest that there is more inside than the viewer can see.

Adding shades and/or curtains is another way to create an illusion. Make a shade by gluing a piece of plain brown paper, cut from a paper bag, to the inside of the window. Make a small pull cord from wire or thread. When installing shades, set them at different heights to add interest; some could even be crooked or torn. (Note: I've found that snails like to eat paper. If your building is not sealed from critters, coat the paper with silicone to protect it.) Simulate curtains with lace or ribbon, found at fabric stores.

Simulate open Venetian blinds with very thin horizontal lines across the window. Press white tape onto a piece of acrylic. Then, using a ruler, draw thin lines. You can also cut lines into the tape with a sharp, pointed tool, such as a scriber or hobby knife. Open the cut line just enough to allow light to pass, simulating partially open blinds. To suggest tightly closed blinds, overlap thin strips of tape. Evergreen Scale Models HO scale clapboard also looks like closed blinds. Cut a piece of material to fit your window and glue in place. You could use all these methods on the same building to suggest blinds that are set differently in each window.

To protect the blinds from the weather, place another sheet of clear acrylic over the backside of the first one. This "laminating" method can also be used to protect other decorations, such as lettering or signs.

Adding details

A simple way to suggest a full interior is to make a "shadow box." Build a false wall behind a window and dress it up with suitable details. This works especially well in a storefront. For example, if you have a grocery store, you could display food items in the store window (**fig. 5**). Theatrical tricks can create a feeling of depth. If your building does not have an interior, paint the inside of the structure black. (If there is an interior, paint it a light color.) Black absorbs the light. If you use a shadow box in conjunction with a black interior,

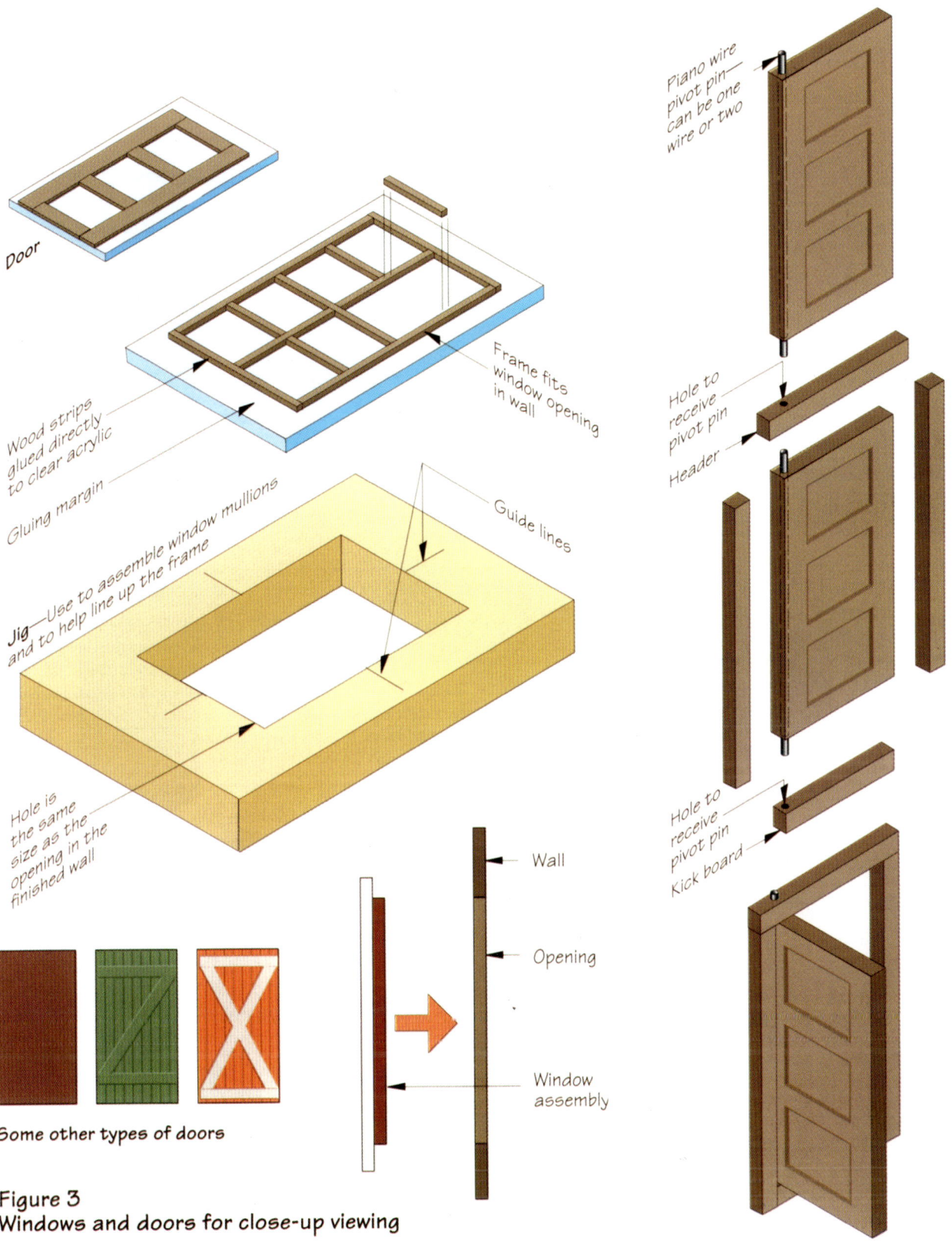

Figure 3
Windows and doors for close-up viewing

Figure 4
A simple hinge for doors

The B. Walter Hardware & Supply building features shadow boxes in the front windows to suggest an interior. The windows, doors, and trim for this structure are cast resin.

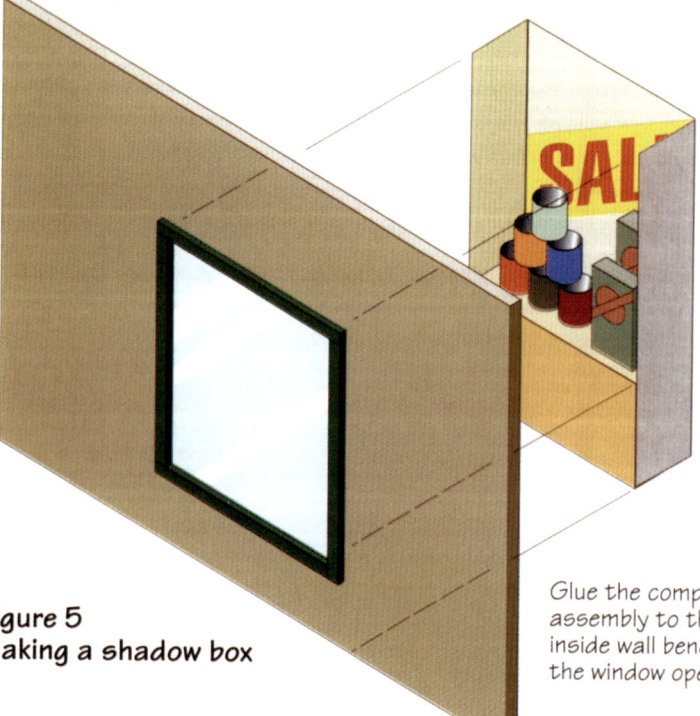

Make the block to match the distance between the floor and the window sill, and make it the width of the opening.

Add details to the completed box

Figure 5
Making a shadow box

Glue the complete assembly to the inside wall beneath the window opening

the shadow box will stand out and the rest of the interior will recede.

Light the areas you want to see. If you place a light over the shadow box, your details will be noticed. When placing lights, however, make sure the light fixture itself is hidden from view. As a general rule, you want to see the light but not the source. See chapter 15.

A trick we used in our Crystal Springs Hotel was to add silhouettes, made from black paper, to the backsides of the shades, which were drawn. This building is illuminated, so at night you see the silhouettes through the shades.

Another simple way to suggest life is to place items in the window or on the sills. A flower pot, a cat in the window, or a bird cage hanging in the window will create the illusion that there is more inside.

Door details

Doors can be detailed too. Make door handles or knobs from brass wire, brads, or round-head pins. Ready-made door knobs, with a plate and key, can be purchased from dollhouse or miniatures suppliers. Other items that might be added to doors are knockers, mail slots, dummy hinges, and seasonal decorations.

I usually like to have my doors closed, because the structures are outside and I want to prevent unwanted visitors from entering. However, doors can be made to open and close. Small hinges are available from companies such as Houseworks. You can also make a simple hinge from a piece of piano wire (**fig. 4**).

If you make a structure with opening doors, such as a barn or garage, you can detail the insides of the doors with items such as tools, license plates, and signs.

SOURCES

Houseworks Ltd.
2388 Pleasantdale Rd.
Atlanta, GA 30340
www.houseworksltd.com

Testor Corp.
www.testors.com

Plastic fabrication

CHAPTER 8

Plastic is a versatile model-building material that can be used to make a wide variety of detail parts. Unlike wood, plastic has no grain and is even easier to work with. When protected from sunlight (such as with paint), it is weatherproof.

Texture is important. Some ABS plastic sheets have one side that is textured. I used this side to simulate stucco. I fabricated the shingles from 120-grit wet/dry sandpaper. I cut the sandpaper into strips with notches, and attached them with tape adhesive. Using a mixture of spray paints to give color variation, I painted the strips prior to assembly.

Here ¼" ABS plastic has been cut out. ABS cuts easily with the same tools that you would use for plywood.

The walls are cemented together using Weld-on 2354, applied with a syringe bottle. Small triangular pieces are used in the corners mainly to keep the wall square. If the proper glue is used, no additional reinforcing is needed.

All the walls have been joined.

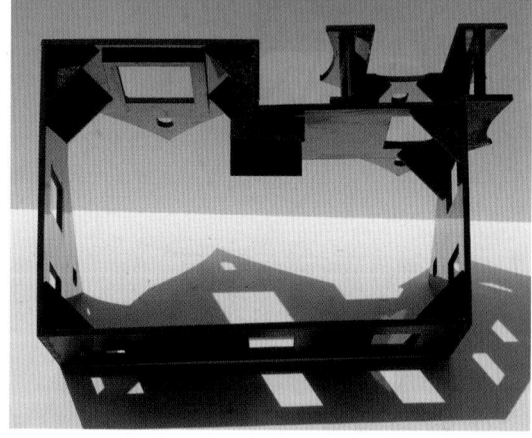
The bracing shown here is mainly for alignment.

In chapters 6 and 7 we discussed wood as a material to make detailed, three-dimensional window mullions. Wood's primary drawback is deterioration, especially when cut to the small sizes required in making models.

Plastic provides crisp, clean parts that can be made to look like almost any prototype material (such as wood or metal). This is important for structures that will be viewed up close, or structures that you may want to photograph close-up or enter in a model contest.

Trim parts, moldings, and other elements—even entire buildings—can be made from plastic. Those of you who read model railroading magazines such as *Garden Railways* and *Model Railroader* have seen how well plastic works for kitbashing and scratchbuilding locomotives and rolling stock. There is really no limit to what you can do with this material.

For those who would like a handbook dedicated exclusively to styrene fabrication, one is available from Evergreen Scale Models.

Hobby shops stock several types of plastic suitable for outdoor structures. The most widely available are styrene and ABS. ABS is stronger than styrene, but more brittle and a bit harder to glue. However, these plastics can be used together and interchangeably.

The two main suppliers of these materials in sizes for model making are Evergreen Scale Models and Plastruct. Evergreen makes a wide variety of sizes and shapes. The company offers strip material ranging from .010" x .020" to .250"-square in lengths of 14" and 24". Also available from Evergreen are structural shapes such as I-beams and tubing, as well as 6" x 12" and 12" x 24" sheets of varying thicknesses, both smooth and textured in various patterns. Most textured sheet materials are designed for HO or O scale, but some of these materials can be used on large-scale models for things like simulated Venetian blinds and vent grills.

Plastruct also makes structural shapes such as I-beams, angles, tubes, square stock, and small sheets in ABS and styrene. The company makes detail items such as ladders and railings, pipe fittings, dummy pumps, dummy valves, parts to make storage tank models, and many other parts. Many Plastruct accessories, including theater seats, open umbrellas for tables, and textured sheet materials, are useful to modelers. Some

Plastruct products are made of styrene, but most of the structural shapes are ABS.

Both companies offer clear styrene sheets. Note: some clear styrene will yellow in the outdoor environment; clear acrylic will not. Styrene plastic can also be purchased in sheets as large as 4' x 8', in various thicknesses. These can be found at local plastics suppliers. They are useful for making large parts such as walls for complete structures.

In my opinion, all modelers should have catalogs from Plastruct and Evergreen Scale Models in their workshops.

Here is quick guide to plastics available in sheets suitable for making structures:

ABS (Acrylonitrile Butadiene Styrene) is available in sheets from .040" thick up to more than an inch thick. It is also available in structural shapes for model making. Some ABS comes with a textured side that's great for roofs and simulated stucco finished walls.

Acrylic (polymethyl methacrylate) is commonly known by the Plexiglas brand name. This material is available in sheets in a variety of thicknesses ranging from 1/16" to more than an inch. For structures, acrylic is ideal for use as window glazing or walls.

It is a bit tricky to work with when it comes to drilling and cutting. When using a table saw to cut acrylic, the resulting dust is hot: Wear eye and face protection.

PVC (polyvinyl chloride) is available in sheets ranging from 1/16" to more than an inch thick. It is also available in a foam-board form that is especially well-suited for garden railway structure walls or other components that require cutting openings. It's also handy for bases and roof substructures.

PVC is easy to cut and does not have the melting problem encountered with styrene when openings are cut with a scroll saw. When using a table saw to cut PVC, the sawdust is less of a problem than with acrylic. However, you should still wear eye and face protection. The foam type cuts easily with a hobby knife, and its surface can be scribed.

Styrene (polystyrene, also known as vinyl benzene) is available from Evergreen and Plastruct in dimensional strips as well as hundreds of shapes and

A 1/16"-thick ABS roof is glued in place. Aluminum duct tape is used as flashing.

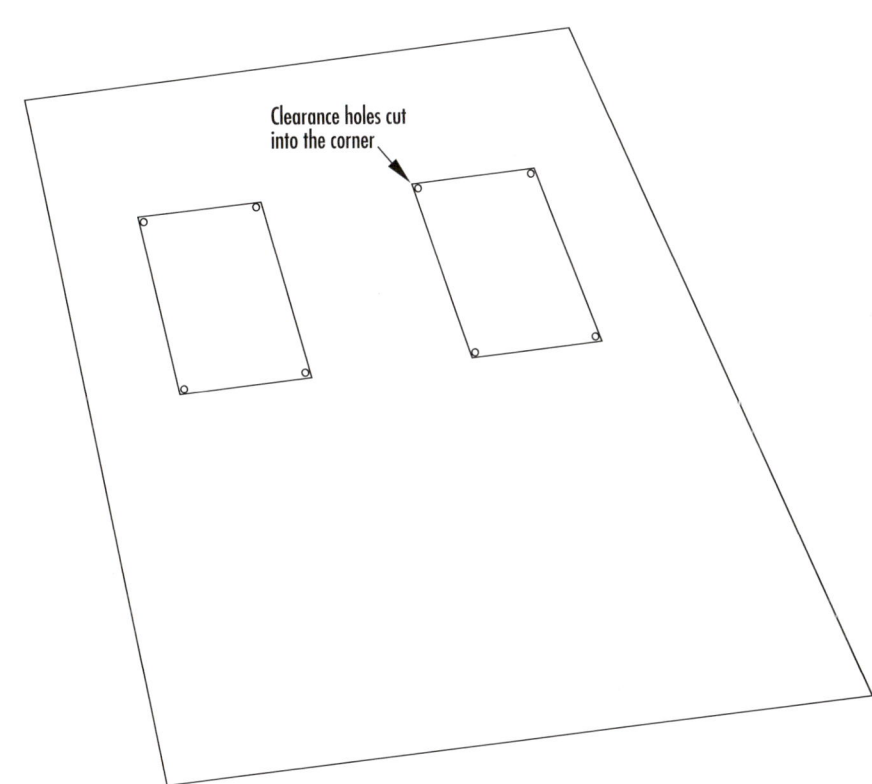

ABS fabrication

This water wheel demonstrates the versatility of styrene and ABS plastics and their ability to withstand the elements. Except for the axle, the entire wheel assembly was made from 1/8"-thick styrene cut from sheet stock (see drawing). MEK bonded the parts, and the unit was painted with Floquil. This wheel has been outside at least four years. Being a water wheel, it is wet all the time and has shown no sign of separation at any of its many seams.

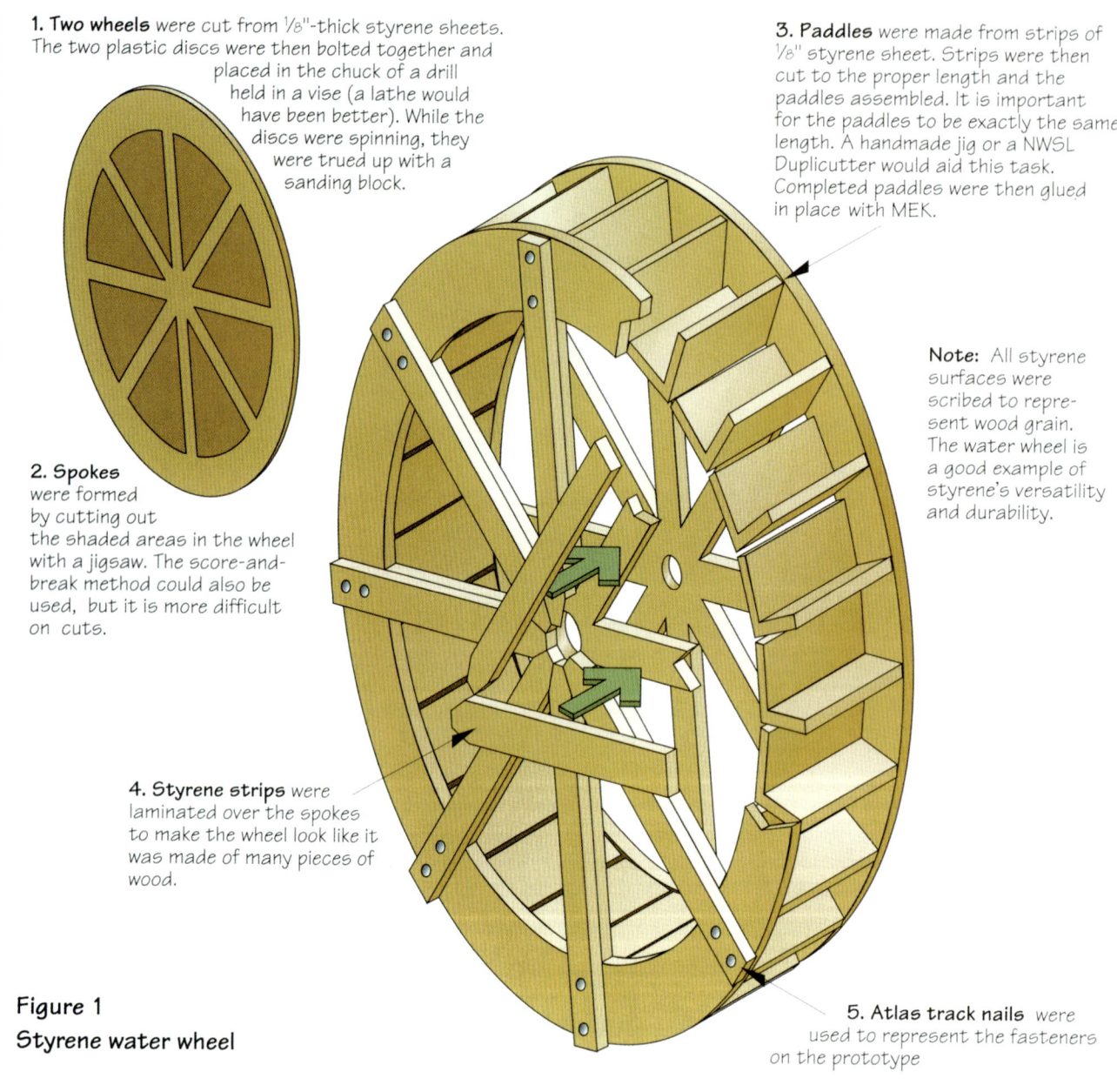

1. Two wheels were cut from 1/8"-thick styrene sheets. The two plastic discs were then bolted together and placed in the chuck of a drill held in a vise (a lathe would have been better). While the discs were spinning, they were trued up with a sanding block.

2. Spokes were formed by cutting out the shaded areas in the wheel with a jigsaw. The score-and-break method could also be used, but it is more difficult on cuts.

3. Paddles were made from strips of 1/8" styrene sheet. Strips were then cut to the proper length and the paddles assembled. It is important for the paddles to be exactly the same length. A handmade jig or a NWSL Duplicutter would aid this task. Completed paddles were then glued in place with MEK.

Note: All styrene surfaces were scribed to represent wood grain. The water wheel is a good example of styrene's versatility and durability.

4. Styrene strips were laminated over the spokes to make the wheel look like it was made of many pieces of wood.

5. Atlas track nails were used to represent the fasteners on the prototype

Figure 1
Styrene water wheel

sizes including beams, tubing, channels, trim parts, window mullions, window and door frames, doors, and a variety of other small parts suitable for model making.

Styrene also comes in sheets up to 4' x 8' in a variety of thicknesses. In sheet form, it can be used for walls, roofs, bracing, and to make a variety of structures and substructures.

It is difficult to cut sheet styrene with a scroll saw because of the heat caused by the cutting process. The saw melts the plastic, sealing the blade in the work as it is cut. Cut openings by hand with a coping saw to prevent this.

When using a table saw to cut styrene, the sawdust is hot. Wear eye and face protection. Openings can also be made by scoring the material. Mark out and score the area to be cut. Drill a hole in each corner and the center and then score the area from the corner to the center hole. You will end up with

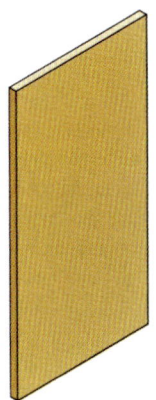  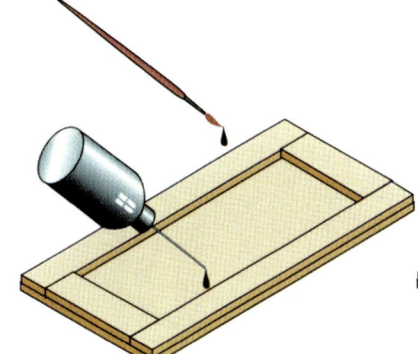 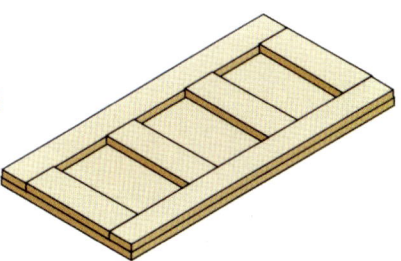

1. Cut styrene sheet stock to size to form the door's base

2. Cut styrene strips to frame door panel

3. Apply a few drops of cement with a syringe bottle or brush. Capillary action will take the glue into the joints. Use tweezers to hold parts in place.

4. Additional panels can be added if desired

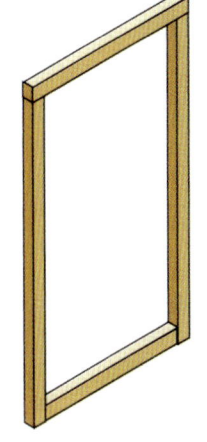  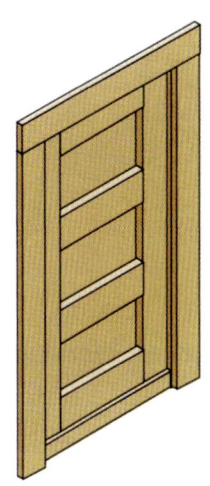

Figure 2
Styrene door construction

5. Construct a frame from styrene strip to fit door

6. Add door molding

7. Glue door into frame

four triangular sections. Push them out one at a time.

Cutting

Plastic can be cut by scoring it. To cut strips to length, score the material where you want the cut. If the material is thin, you may only need one or two strokes. Thicker material may require a few more passes. In some cases, as in larger square-section stock, it may be necessary to rotate the strip and score two or three sides, then snap it. If the end is not square, you can use a knife to square it off.

Scoring should be done with a scoring tool, not a razor knife. A scoring tool cuts a "V" groove and removes the material—a knife does not. The Chopper tool, sold by NorthWest Short Line, easily cuts small plastic strips to length.

To cut sheets of flat stock, use the scoring method. With a metal straightedge as a guide, score the material several times until it is cut approximately one-quarter of the way through. Lay the cut line along the corner of a table and snap it. Although a razor saw, or any fine-tooth saw, can be used to cut this material, scoring the material is the cleanest, quickest, and easiest.

If you buy a large sheet of plastic, use a table saw to cut the plastic into smaller, more workable pieces. Cutting plastic with a table saw is pretty straightforward. Use caution, the flying sawdust from this material is like a sand blaster and it is hot. Wear eye and face protection.

If you use a jigsaw or scroll saw to cut an intricate pattern or a circle, you may find that the saw blade melts the styrene, causing the cut edge to rejoin behind the blade. Then you'll find your saw blade stuck in the middle of a piece of styrene with no way to get out. (This is not a problem with straight cuts on the table saw because of the wide kerf left by the blade.) To avoid this, cut slowly. Keep a container of water nearby to cool the blade periodically. I have also heard of using a stream of air to keep the blade cool. This problem can be avoided completely buy using

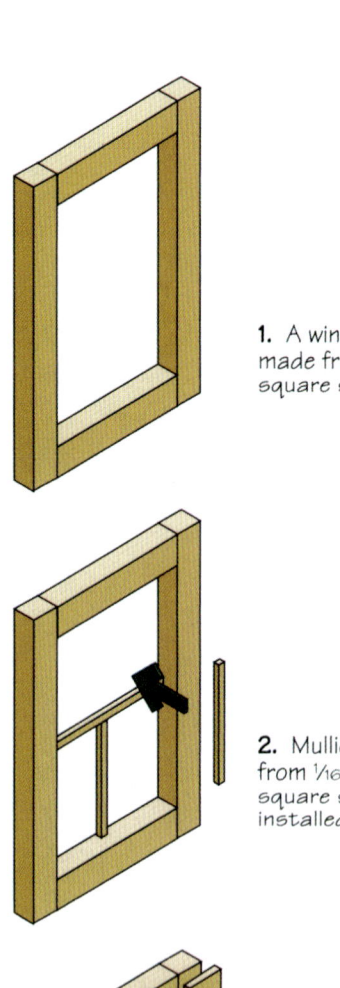
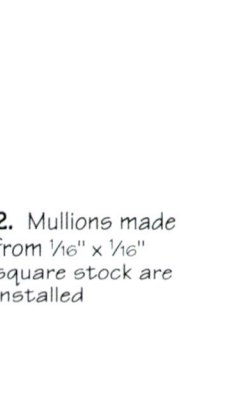
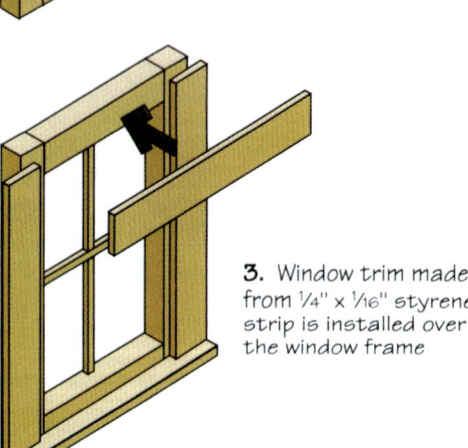

1. A window frame is made from ¼" x ¼" square stock

2. Mullions made from ⅟₁₆" x ⅟₁₆" square stock are installed

3. Window trim made from ¼" x ⅟₁₆" styrene strip is installed over the window frame

Double-hung windows can be made with two windows in a single frame. The top window overlaps the bottom, as shown, and should be the outermost window of the two. With skill and care, these can be made to open.

Figure 3—Styrene window construction

another type of plastic for items, such as walls, that need openings cut out. This will be covered in more detail later in this chapter.

Gluing plastic

Plastics are bonded to themselves using solvent type cements. See chapter 2 for details.

When using plastic for garden-railroad applications, it may be necessary to bond other materials to it such as wood, metal, concrete, or foam. Since MEK and other solvent-based cements work by melting and welding the material, they will not work on non-plastic materials. You must use another type of glue, such as epoxy, Quick Grab, or E6000.

Making basic doors and windows

Now that we've learned the basics, let's make something. I will start with smaller components that can be used as part of a structure. The basic methods are the same whether you are making a small part or a complete structure.

This section is not intended to repeat the chapter on making doors and windows, but be a step-by-step exercise in the use of styrene, illustrated by constructing doors and windows. Styrene strips as available from Evergreen Models and Plastruct are well suited for making doors, window,s and all sorts of trim and decorative pieces. For me, it is not worth the time and effort it takes to cut styrene or ABS sheets into strips from sheet material, so I use precut styrene strip.

When working on these projects, keep your work flat and use a clean, level surface. To prevent glue from sticking to your work surface, cover the surface with waxed paper or work on a piece of glass.

Simple door

Let's start with a door (page 55). First, cut a piece of styrene or ABS sheet to the size of a door, say a scale 7' high by 30" wide. Thickness is not critical here; plus or minus a sixteenth of an inch is OK. This will be the door's core.

Next, using ⅟₁₆" x ¼" plastic strip, lay out a door-panel frame on top of the door's core. To create a wood texture, use a knife or razor saw to scratch the grain on the surface. Knot holes can be made with a scribe, or even drilled with a small bit. After adding wood grain, lay the frame back on the base. Use a pair of tweezers or another metal tool to hold the plastic in place, and apply a little cement to the edges. Capillary action will pull the glue under the piece. When complete, you will have a single-panel door. You can add additional panels using the same technique.

Make a door frame from ¼" x ¼" strips to form a threshold, and ⅛" x ⅟₁₆" strip material for the door moldings. Add additional details, such as door handles and door knockers, if desired.

Remember that the measurements used here for doors and windows are nominal. You can substitute smaller or larger strips depending on your application and scale.

Simple window

You can build a window using a similar method. Glue ¼" x ¼" strip stock together to form a window frame. At this point, your assembly will look like a picture frame. Seams rarely show. In fact, if you want a seam or joint to show, you may have to cut it in later with a knife or saw. See the drawings on page 56.

Add mullions cut from 1/16" x 1/16" strips. A simple window has a single horizontal crossbar only, creating an upper and lower windowpane. Create a more common four-light window by adding additional pieces to divide the window vertically. This may sound complicated, but remember, plastic does not have grain and is very easy to cut, trim, and glue. Unlike wood, it does not splinter or split. Add a frame around the window, and the insert the window into the interior opening. Styrene strips and shapes can also be used to make window trim, molding, siding, stairways, railings, bricks, shingles, and just about anything else you can imagine. The absence of grain makes styrene a good material to carve. You can make gingerbread trim, decorative knees, porch railings, fences, and other things. All can be made weatherproof by painting.

If you need several identical parts, such as windows, doors, or trim pieces, there is one drawback to this method—the time it takes to make these parts individually. For example, if you are making a structure that needs 32 windows and six doors, you might be cutting plastic for hours. In chapter 13 I describe how to cast duplicate parts from resin.

Plastic structures

You can make a variety of components out of plastic strips, even entire buildings. The largest parts of a building are the roof and walls. Most walls have at least one window or door opening in them. These openings present a challenge in making walls out of styrene, in that it's difficult to cut an opening in sheet styrene.

Avoid this problem by not cutting out openings, but rather building your wall up in pieces, leaving the window areas open. You can use relatively large panels, cementing them together. You can also build up a wall in the same way as a full-size building, using a frame and planks.

Acrylic has similar problems as styrene in that it's difficult to cut out window and door openings. If you use clear acrylic, avoid cutting by using the acrylic wall itself as the window or door. Make a window frame and mullions as illustrated above, then glue the window directly on the acrylic sheet in the proper place. Mask the parts that will be the window glazing. You can either sheath walls with planks, or paint the walls, leaving the window and door glass unpainted.

General tips on plastic

When you build a structure, you are making a structurally sound box.

GUIDE TO CEMENTING DISSIMILAR PLASTICS

PVC to PVC
Weld-On 2007

PVC to styrene:
IPS #16
Plastic Weld

PVC to ABS
IPS #16
Plastic Weld

PVC to acrylic
IPS #16
Plastic Weld

ABS to ABS
Weld-on 2354
MEK

ABS to acrylic
IPS #16
Plastic Weld

ABS to PVC I
PS #16
Plastic Welder

ABS to styrene
MEK
IPS #16

Acrylic to acrylic
Weld-on 3 or 4
IPS #16

Acrylic to styrene
Weld-On 3
IPS #16

Acrylic to PVC
IPS #16

Acrylic to ABS
IPS #16

Styrene to styrene
MEK
IPS #16

Styrene to PVC
IPS #16
Plastic Welder

Styrene to ABS
MEK
IPS #16

Styrene to acrylic
Weld-On 3
IPS #16

See chapter 3 on Tools for special tools for working with plastic.

SOURCES FOR STYRENE

Evergreen Scale Models
12808 N.E. 125th Way
Kirkland, WA 98034
www.evergreenscalemodels.com
Styrene Handbook: $1

Plastruct
1020 S. Wallace Place, Dept. G5
City of Industry, CA 91748
www.plastruct.com
This company has a large catalog (250 pages) of plastic shapes and parts, including a variety of plastic items mainly intended for architectural models. There are even some 1/2"-scale items. Many of the structural materials can be used for large-scale models.

Precision Products
763 Cayuga St., Unit 2
Lewiston, NY 14092-1724
www.appliedimaginationinc.com
Precision Products manufactures plastic-veneer sheets in G scale. The company offers a variety of masonry-type siding, as well as wood-type siding and roofing in vacuum-formed styrene sheets. Veneer is too thin to use structurally, so the manufacturer recommends laminating the sheets to a strong box. The company recommends using a product it calls Perfic Panels Plus, a super white high impact polystyrene skin with a polystyrene foam core. See the website for details. A box made of styrene, ABS, PVC or acrylic will also work.

Always use the proper cements for the plastic you are working with. Do not use silicone or CA glue. When properly bonded, a plastic joint will be as strong as the plastic itself.

Corner braces and internal framing add strength to the structure and keep the walls square. An easy way to brace a building is to add floors and a ceiling. Be sure to allow for lighting wires and stairways if you are detail the interior. For wires, drill a simple hole in the floor or ceiling, or dog ear

Acrylic structures

Fellow garden railroader Ken Martin of Castro Valley, Calif., uses clear acrylic to build a variety of structures for his garden railroad. This is an all-clear-acrylic building, with the doors and windows masked off for painting. He painted the entire structure, then peeled the mask away, leaving clear windows and doors. Ken adds styrene plastic strips to make the window frames.

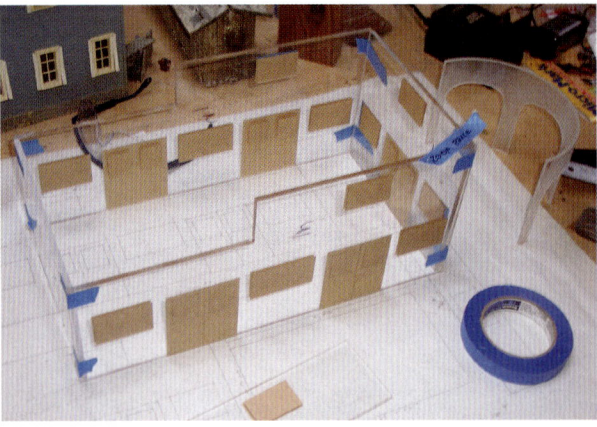

Ken is working on a model of the Berkeley, Calif., station using the technique described above.

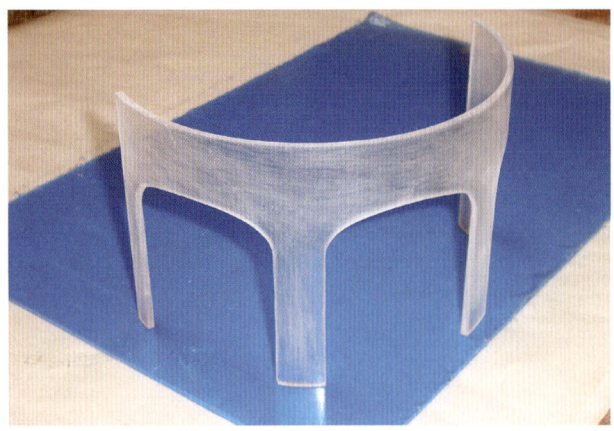

The portico is made from clear acrylic tube. The arches were cut out with a small jigsaw.

The unpainted Berkeley station reveals the materials that have been used. It is all acrylic except for some styrene trim.

The Berkeley station is ready to be placed on the railroad.

Ken also built this model of the Oakland, Calif., station. This has been compressed using some of the methods described in this book.

An L-shaped wood frame works as a jig for keeping acrylic pieces aligned for gluing.

Bonding acrylic

If properly bonded, an acrylic cemented joint will be as strong as the base material. Use only acrylic cement. (The photo at the bottom of page 58 shows an assembly jig designed to hold two pieces in 90-degree alignment.)

Using a hammer, flatten the pointed end of several T-pins. Place the pins under the vertical piece to be glued. The pins create a small gap between the two pieces. Use a syringe applicator and run a line of acrylic cement into the gap.

Let the cement sit for a minute or two. This softens the surfaces to be bonded. Remove the T-pins. Let the pieces cure before handling.

CHECKLIST FOR BUILDING A PLASTIC STRUCTURE

1. Use the correct cement to weld the joints: Weld-on 3 or 4 or IPS No. 16 for acrylic and styrene, Weld-on 2007 for PVC, and Weld-on 2354 for ABS.

2. Before joining plastics, make sure the joint is clean and free of paint, oils etc. Remove burrs and "pre-soften" the material.

3. Use the same plastic to make the entire structural box and its braces. This ensures compatibility, even expansion, and contraction in the joints.

4. Attach dissimilar materials with the proper adhesive, and allow for expansion and contraction. The list below lists material and glues arranged from best down to acceptable.

Wood to plastic
E6000
Epoxy (for small parts)
Tape adhesive
Silicone
Contact cement

Metal to plastic
E6000
Epoxy
Tape adhesive

Dissimilar plastics to each other (see the chart on page 57)

5. Allow glue joints to cure before handling the project.

6. If you need to remove glue residue from silicone or E6000, let the adhesive dry for an hour or longer but less than 12 hours. At that point, you can pick up the edge of the adhesive and peel the excess away.

the corners to allow the wires to pass through.

Corner braces are triangular pieces that fit into the interior corners. A full brace, similar to a floor with the center missing, would allow a floor to be installed later.

Most plastics are smooth. Texture can be added by the addition of plastic battens or planking, or by a scribing tool. This tool removes a thin line of plastic as it is drawn over the material.

ABS is available in black with a rough texture, similar to non-skid surfaces or sandpaper, making it suitable for use as roofing. It is perfect to simulate a flat tar and gravel roof. You could add small battens to simulate the wooden battens nailed down over the seams. Another way to simulate seams is to cut the ABS into strips, then glue the strips to a sub-roof made of a solid sheet of ABS or other compatible plastic.

A miniature saber saw is less aggressive than a full size one, and is well suited for cutting out doors, windows, and arches in acrylic.

CHAPTER 9

Building with Styrofoam and Precision Board

This stone mill has a plywood substructure with an overlayment of thin Styrofoam. I used a stencil cutter and burned random stone patterns into the Styrofoam. I painted the Styrofoam with a base coat of latex, giving each stone a different earth tone. If a coat of latex paint is laid down first, lacquer-base paints can then be used to add color. This particular structure is a composite of different surface finishes. Note the wooden gable (left), wood shingles, wooden addition, and metal roof over the addition.

I wrote the text for the following section about Styrofoam in 1995, and what I said about building garden railway structures with it then still applies today. However, today Precision Board, which is superior in many ways, has nearly become a replacement for Styrofoam. The main advantage of Styrofoam is that it is much less expensive, so it still has its place especially for projects that require a lot of material. And it's readily available—you can even reclaim it from the trash!

Styrofoam (polystyrene thermal insulation) is a versatile building material well suited for use in garden railroads. It is weatherproof when painted and easy to work with. Styrofoam is a trademark name for a foam material manufactured by Dow Chemical Company. Real Styrofoam is the blue board commonly used for building insulation. Coffee cups, fast food containers and ice chests are not actually Styrofoam. They are made from expanded polystyrene beads and do not have the same properties as real Styrofoam. I'll refer to this material as "bead board."

Styrofoam is somewhat more expensive than bead board, but is stronger and easier to etch with a soldering iron or stencil cutter (more on this later). Bead board make a bigger mess when it is cut with a saw, as it tends to break apart along the edges. It is better to cut it with a hot wire or hot knife.

I learned about real Styrofoam after I had already used bead board to build most of my older foam-based structures. In some cases, I used recycled meat-packaging trays. These foam trays are denser than regular bead board and they are thin, making them ideal for specific jobs. I used this thin foam as a covering over plywood walls.

Styrofoam for garden-railroad buildings

Styrofoam and beadboard can be used in several ways to build model structures. To make a basic structural box, glue four walls together with water-based contact cement. Add a wooden brace to the inside corners for additional gluing surface. You can add corner trim to the outside corners later for a finished look.

Plastic or wood corners are available from your local hobby shop, or you can make them from strip material. Next, glue wood planks to the foam with a water-based contact cement. Apply the contact cement to the wood and the Styrofoam. Allow the cement to dry to the touch. Test it by touching the cement. If it sticks to your finger, it's not ready yet. Once it is dried, place the wood strips on the Styrofoam.

The reverse of this "building core" method is to build a plywood shell and cover the exterior with Styrofoam. I have done this often to replicate stone, brick, or other special material. In these cases, I use the foam as a medium for adding texture to a structure, rather than as a structural part of the building.

Another method is to use Styrofoam to create the entire building, both the structural wall and the finished wall. Styrofoam can be made to look like stucco, brick, stone, or adobe, and will accept mortar and other texturing materials. I like to add strength and weight with wood bracing on the inside of Styrofoam structures. Toothpicks can be used to hold walls together while test fitting.

This it the water mill several years after construction. The original wooden roof deteriorated from the weather, so it was replaced with a cast-resin roof. The original walls are still going strong.

This roundhouse was my first Styrofoam building. The basic structure is made of plywood. I glued pieces of Styrofoam, cut from meat-packing trays, to the plywood substructure and carved them with a soldering iron to represent dressed stone. Then, I painted the entire structure with latex paint. Note that individual stones were highlighted in shades of gray, brown, and charcoal.

Basic styrofoam construction

Wood or stucco can be applied over the styrofoam core. Titebond II glue works well for wood.

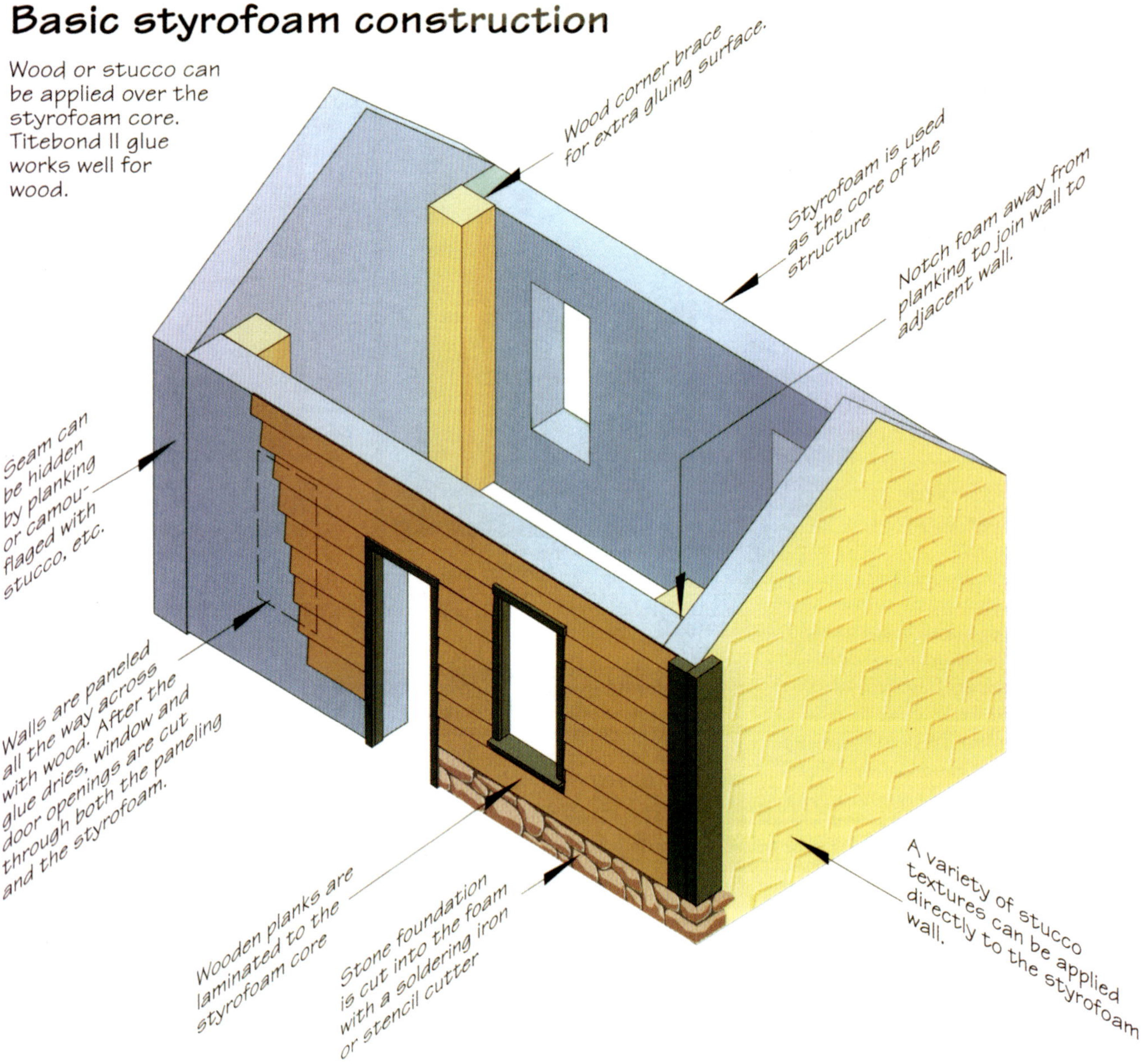

Wood corner brace for extra gluing surface.

Styrofoam is used as the core of the structure

Notch foam away from planking to join wall to adjacent wall.

Seam can be hidden by planking or camouflaged with stucco, etc.

Walls are paneled all the way across with wood. After the glue dries, window and door openings are cut through both the paneling and the styrofoam.

Wooden planks are laminated to the styrofoam core

Stone foundation is cut into the foam with a soldering iron or stencil cutter

A variety of stucco textures can be applied directly to the styrofoam wall.

Stone patterns
These are a small sample of the dozens of different commonly used stone patterns.

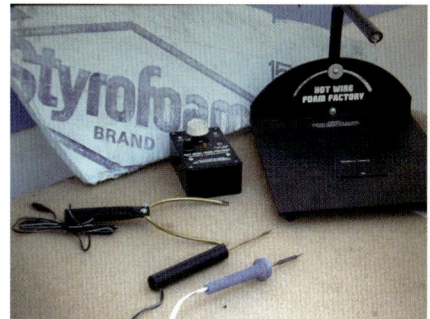

The Hot Wire Foam Factory is a set of tools designed for working with Styrofoam. The large table works similar to a scroll saw. The wishbone device carves scenery and the stylus etches in details. All tools are powered by a variable transformer.

Working with Styrofoam

Cutting: You can cut Styrofoam with just about anything that cuts wood or plastic. Professionals use a special hot-wire machine, which cuts clean and fast. Hot-wire cutters are sold at some hobby shops.

Cutting tools commonly available to the average hobbyist are the table saw, jigsaw, scroll saw, electric kitchen knife, and hobby knife. These tools also cut bead board, but be prepared to clean up a mess. Have a vacuum cleaner handy to suck up debris as the material is cut. To prevent this mess, I strongly recommend the hot wire cutting method.

Another tool that can be used to cut Styrofoam is a soldering iron. Getting a straight, even cut can be a bit tricky. However, with practice and the proper touch, you can cut a fairly straight edge. The soldering iron is a good tool for cutting out windows and doors.

Gluing. You must use glues that are specifically designed for Styrofoam. The best one that I have found is Fasthond Contact Cement by 3M, a water-based contact cement.

Painting. You cannot paint Styrofoam or bead board with solvent-based pants, as they will eat through the foam. The best choice is a water-based latex or acrylic paint. For detail work, I use Floquil's Polly S, a water-based hobby paint that flows well into thin cracks or mortar joints. For plain surfaces, I use latex house paint. Although Styrofoam is not biodegradable, it will weather if not protected by paint. It can be affected by UV radiation, becoming brittle on the surface, so it's a good idea to protect it with a coat of paint.

Texturing: A nice feature of Styrofoam is that it can be easily textured. Latex house paint is heavy enough that it can be brushed to look like stucco or adobe. For a rougher stucco or adobe finish, you can apply mortar or actual stucco to the surface.

Stone can be imitated nicely with Styrofoam. I carve or melt in mortar lines with a stencil cutter, a tool similar to a soldering iron with a special tip, or a small soldering iron. While the

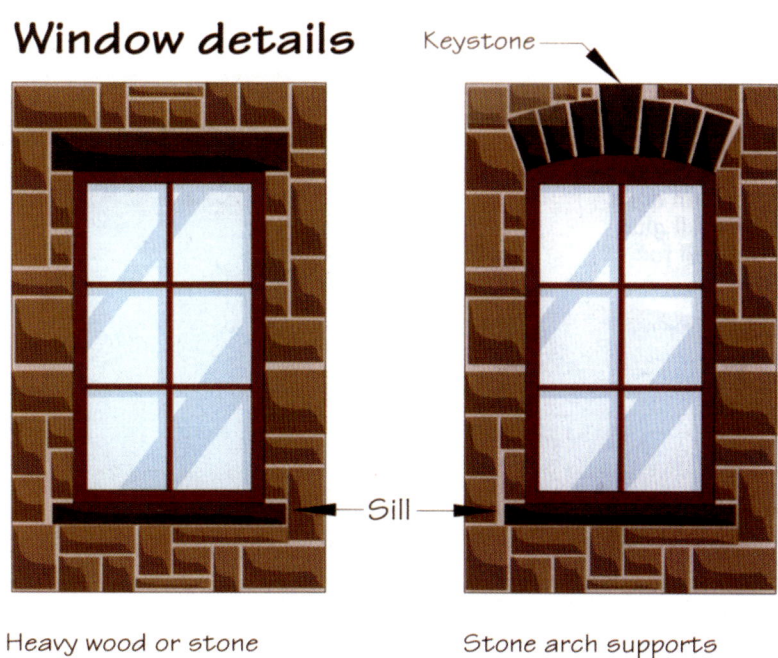

Window details

Heavy wood or stone lintel supports rockwork above window

Stone arch supports rockwork above window

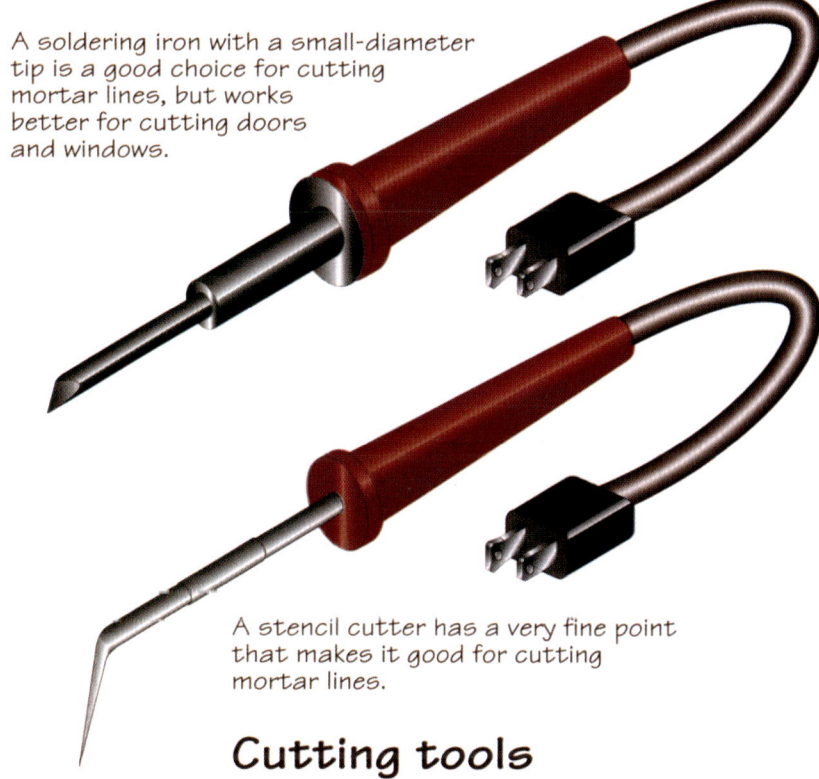

A soldering iron with a small-diameter tip is a good choice for cutting mortar lines, but works better for cutting doors and windows.

A stencil cutter has a very fine point that makes it good for cutting mortar lines.

Cutting tools

Brick texture looks good on many structures, and the texture can be easily added to Precision Board or foam before painting.

Rainbow Ridge offers a variety of kits as well as Precision Board parts such as wall material in large scale.

two tools differ in the shape and size of their tips, the end result is similar (see page 62). Use the stencil cutter or soldering iron as you would a pencil, then melt in the mortar lines. It takes practice to get the best results. If done too slowly, you will melt away too much Styrofoam.

Use different patterns to replicate the type of stonework you want. Typical patterns include uniform dressed stone, random dressed stone, undressed stone, rubble, brick (Brick is difficult to simulate in ½" scale because of the width of the cuts made by the tool), cinder or concrete building block, and round rock. Added texture can be created by roughing up the surface with the edge of a cutter.

Carving. Styrofoam can be carved easily, making the formation of irregular shapes, such as domes or arches, a simple task. A wood rasp or similar cutting tool works well for this purpose.

Coffee cups. My first experience with foam as a model-building material was with a foam coffee cup, torn into pieces that were glued to a wooden base to make a stone chimney. The result was convincing. (As I mentioned earlier, you can also use discarded meat trays. These are made of a thin, dense foam that makes them good for laminating to a wood base.)

Making thin sheets of foam. Make thin foam sheets on a table saw or band saw by cutting off strips, just as you would with wood. Laminate these strips to wood shells and texture them as desired. This technique can be used to change the look of an existing building, for example, if you've built a wooden building that you would like to turn into a stone building. Glue Styrofoam strips onto the walls, then carve and texture them for a new look. You can also buy thin Styrofoam sheets at hobby shops. These are often sold as a model airplane building material.

There is no limit to what you can do with this material. I've used Styrofoam for tunnel portals and as molds for concrete bridges and viaducts.

Precision Board

Precision Board (PB) is a high-density urethane that has been used commercially since 1964. It has no grain and it is dimensionally stable. When UV protected, it is weatherproof. The material can be carved with basic woodworking or hobby tools such as a hobby knife, scribe, or awl, and a wire brush can be used to create wood-grain patterns. Unlike Styrofoam, you cannot cut it with a hot wire or hot knife.

PB must be glued with polyurethane glue or CA glue in gel form, and it must be painted on both sides to prevent it from warping.

In ½" sheets, PB is strong enough to build a small structure without bracing. Larger structures should be braced on the interior.

Carving in texture is easy. Choose a tool you are comfortable with, such as an awl, scribe, dental pick, or motor tool-powered stylus. Create texture with a wire brush.

Some modelers build everything out of this material, including simulated wood-grained planks, log walls, and wood shingled roofs, as well as stone and bricks. I prefer it for rock and masonry work. When used to imitate wood, I think the texture is too heavy.

Precision Board is especially well suited for use as a structure base. The edges can be finished to look like cement, brick, cement blocks, stone or any other texture. You can texture both the edges and the horizontal surface. It is easy to make walkways and planting areas by cutting away the material. You can create a complete platform to set your buildings on.

SOURCE
Rainbow Ridge
Lakeside, California
Phone: 619-561-0643
rainbowridgekits@aol.com
RRkits@aol.com
www.rainbowridgekits.com

This shop building is made of Precision Board into which brick and stone block patterns have been carved.

Even this overpass was made from Precision Board. The board's natural texture lends itself well to simulating cement.

Pauline's Tea House is patterned after a real storybook-type building in Carmel, Calif. The simulated thatch roof was shaped out of Magic Sculp.

CHAPTER 10

Magic Sculp epoxy putty

Magic Sculp can be used for a variety of structure projects. It is an epoxy putty with two parts combined in a 1:1 ratio. You knead it like dough, then work the material like modeling clay. You can shape it by hand or with basic sculpting tools to create almost any shape. The material stays pliable for about an hour before it begins to harden. You can work the material anytime during the curing period and even after it is cured. The cured material will become nearly as hard as rock and, when painted, is weatherproof.

During the early curing stage, you can use water to shape and smooth the material, similar to the way you would work modeling clay. You can work the material into any shape or texture—and any size. The material's grain is fine, and once cured, the product will not shrink or crack.

Magic Sculp differs from products like Sculpy and Fimo, which are polymer clays that must be cured in an oven. Magic Sculp cures at room temperature. You don't have to worry about fitting your project in to an oven. It cures by chemical reaction, so it will cure even under water.

The working time depends on the temperature. It cures faster in warm weather than in cool weather. In almost any condition, you will have a minimum of an hour of working time. You can add new layers to cured material, so you can work with small amounts at a time if you are making a larger piece. If you choose to add a new layer to a cured piece, I suggest you make a series of holes in the first part to give the new layer more surface grip.

Magic Sculp will stick to most plastics and wood, and I have used it to bond parts together. When I wanted to install Accucraft knuckle couplers on my Bachmann cars, I used Magic Sculp to attach the draft gear. The Magic Sculp preformed two functions—it became the shim or mounting bracket for the draft gear, and it bonded the draft gear to the car. I did install one screw, mainly to hold the coupler together.

Magic Sculp can be stored indefinately. The manufacturer suggests softening unmixed material in the microwave before working with it. I normally use it out of the container at room temperature. Heated material will cure faster.

If I need an item that's an odd shape, I use Magic Sculp. On Pauline's Tea House (a storybook-type structure), I needed a replica of a simulated thatch roof. The full-size building had an interesting curved shape covered with wood shingles. I made the basic roof out of styrene and hand-molded the curved section out of Magic Sculp. To ensure adhesion to the styrene, I roughed up the edges of the styrene to create some tooth. I applied aluminum

Here Magic Sculp camouflages a sprinkler. The riser pipe was covered with Magic Sculp, then made to look like a dead tree.

The seven dwarfs' cottage is an old structure. Originally, it had a straw roof made from a broom. That roof was replaced with one made from Magic Sculp.

About Magic Sculp

- It's an epoxy putty that has the working characteristics of modeling clay.
- It can be sculpted into any shape.
- You can use water to smooth it.
- Since it cures chemically, it hardens without having to be baked.
- It will cure under water.
- The finished project can be made thin or thick and will not crack.
- Once cured, it is nearly as hard as rock.
- When painted to protect it from UV light, it will be weatherproof.
- Cured material can be sanded; you can grind, polish, or thread it.
- It will bond to a variety of materials.
- You can use talcum powder to prevent bonding.
- Un-mixed material has a long shelf life.
- It has a working time of an hour or longer before it hardens.

Magic Sculp comes in two parts and is the consistency of modeling clay. Once kneaded together, it will begin to harden. Within 24 hours, it becomes rock hard.

While not pretty, a functional motor mount was made using Magic Sculp. Masking tape was wrapped around the motor so it would not stick to the Magic Sculp motor mount. Two screws hold down a strap.

The Three Little Pigs' house, originally made from straw, eventually rotted away, so I made a new one using Magic Sculp. This material is stronger than the brick house, but don't tell the Big Bad Wolf.

duct tape over the styrene and the Magic Sculp to make the shingles.

I built a seven dwarfs' cottage several years ago with a thatch roof made out of an old straw broom. Over the years, this rotted away, so I made a new roof out of Magic Sculp. The basic roof is styrene, with Magic Sculp applied over that. I used my fingers and a comb to make a simulated thatch roof. This roof is now several years old and shows no sign of wear.

Magic Sculp can be used to camouflage items. I made my sprinkler's riser pipe look like a tree trunk. First, I roughened the surface of the pipe with sandpaper. I applied Magic Sculp to the pipe, creating a tree-bark texture. When I mixed the Magic Sculp, I added in a little brown acrylic paint, almost like a color primer to make it easier to color later on.

The uses for Magic Sculp are many; the only limitation is your imagination.

SOURCES

TAP Plastics
www.tapplastics.com
(TAP Plastics retail stores can be found in parts of the West.)

Wesco Enterprises
3235 Monier Circle, Suite 1
Ranch Cordova, CA 95742
www.magicsculp.com

Casting resin parts for your buildings

CHAPTER 11

The Crystal Springs Hotel is made entirely of homemade resin castings and styrene plastic. It is a scratchbuilt, one-of-a-kind building. Even though cast materials were used, there is no mold for the building itself—just molds for the wall and the roof materials. This building can be left outdoors safely.

Although styrene is great for modeling, the material can be time-consuming to work with when mass-producing parts. If, for example, you need several of the same piece, it takes a lot of time to create each piece from scratch. The next logical step is to make molds and cast these parts in resin.

69

This is an example of one of my ready-made walls. At the top of the photo is the master. I bought wooden clapboard sheets, then built a wall using several sheets of the material. I added a little more wood grain and created seams between the boards to add more detail. Next, I built a mold box creating the finished mold shown.

These are masters of complete facades. The one on the left is a combination of resin and plastic; the one on the right is wood. I made molds of these facades so I could make a number of these buildings.

> **TIPS FOR WORKING WITH RESIN**
> - Work in a well-ventilated, dry area.
> - Keep rags or paper towels handy.
> - Have a trash can standing nearby.
> - Work on a waxed-glass work surface or a piece of waxed particle board.
> - Use popsicle sticks or tongue depressors for mixing.
> - Use a popsicle stick to remove trapped air bubbles from tight places.
> - A postal scale is useful for measuring.
> - Use disposable cups for mixing resin.
> - A plastic mixing pot is best for mixing RTV.
> - Wear gloves or use protective hand cream.

Casting is a simple concept. Anyone who has made ice cubes in a tray or Jell-O in a mold has been introduced to it. You have a mold, and the casting material (water or Jell-O). The mold allows you to duplicate its shape as many times as you like.

The same principle applies to casting parts for the railroad. In this chapter, I will discuss basic open-pour, one-piece molds, with an emphasis on duplicating parts for use on structures. The more complex two-part molds are beyond this chapter, but if you wish to experiment with two-part molds, the basic materials and some of the methods are the same.

Casting parts may not be for everyone. It can be expensive to make parts this way if you need only small quantities, since the rubber used to make molds is costly. If suitable parts are available from a vendor, it is almost always more economical to purchase them ready made. The idea in casting your own parts is to duplicate special items—a set of doors and windows, for example, or special trim parts. Another reason to cast something in resin is if the original part may not be weatherproof. You may be able to make fine items out of bread dough or plaster, but these materials are not weatherproof. By making molds, you can duplicate them in weather-resistant resin.

About molds

Temporary molds can be made from almost anything that will hold your casting medium. A problem is that temporary molds can't always be reused. A real aid to modelers is room-temperature-vulcanizing (RTV) rubber. This material starts out as a liquid the consistency of thick pancake batter. A liquid catalyst is mixed with the raw rubber. After the material has been catalyzed, the curing process begins. Once cured, the material becomes a flexible rubber. The transformation or cure time is usually about 24 hours. Always follow the manufacturer's instructions.

If you use a rigid mold, the parts must be designed with draft (a slight taper) so they can be removed from the mold. Look at a plastic ice-cube tray, and note how the molds are tapered to allow the cubes to release. A great advantage to using RTV rubber is that you don't have to worry about minor undercuts and intricate patterns. The flexible rubber will release the parts by stretching, which means that you do not have to build draft into your original parts.

Rubber molds

There are many types of RTV rubber. The best one is a matter of personal choice. However, there are some limitations based on your equipment. If you do not have a vacuum chamber (to remove air bubbles), for instance, you will be limited to using rubber that will work without one, such as the Bare Metal Foil and Tap Plastics brands of RTV rubber. Both manufacturers claim their products can be used without a vacuum chamber, even though a chamber is recommended (see the sidebar on making a vacuum chamber). Both products are silicone-type rubbers.

Making a mold

Be aware that RTV rubber will pick up any detail that is on the original master, including wood grain, joints, rivets, and even fingerprints. You will have an exact mold of the original master.

The first step in mold making is to build the original, or master, from an easy-to-work material like wood, paper, clay, metal, or plastic. Since we made plastic doors and windows in Chapter 9, we will use them as our masters. Avoid molding items with large undercuts, because bubbles from trapped air will form and the parts will be difficult to remove from the mold.

Since our master is styrene, we will also use styrene to make a mold box. See the drawing at right. Glue the backside of the window to a sheet of styrene. In open-pour molding there will always be a surface that is unmolded. This is the open side, the side where the casting material is poured into the mold. It will not have detail. In our example, the backside of the window is the open side, which is glued to the base of the mold box. There cannot be any space between the base of the mold box and the molded object. Window mullions, for example, must be glued to the base. If they are not, the rubber will form around them and trap

Here are several masters for making molds of windows, doors, and a wall section.

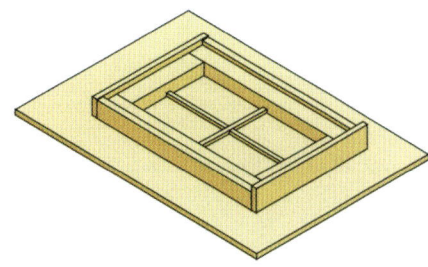

1. Glue the master to a flat base, or build it right on the base. The base will become the bottom of the mold box.

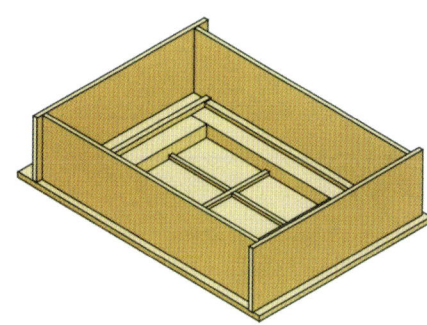

2. When the master is complete, build a watertight dam around it to contain the liquid RTV rubber.

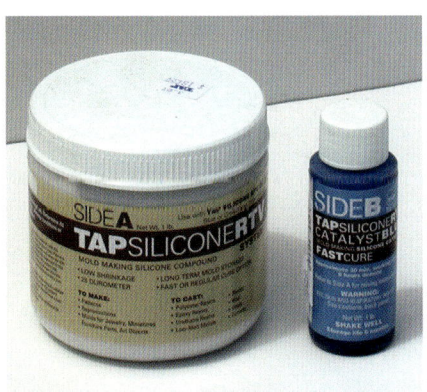

TAP Plastics offers silicone RTV rubber that is catalyzed at 10 percent. A variety of molding rubbers are available. The differences are in the elasticity. Read the instructions for the materials you choose for correct mixing proportions.

Clean modeling clay is a useful material for filling voids in a master, sealing a mold box, or building a "dam" in a mold if you want to pour a smaller part. If you are casting a sheet of clapboard and only want half, you can dam off the mold and pour half. The edge will not be perfect, but you can cut the part square with a saw after the part is cured.

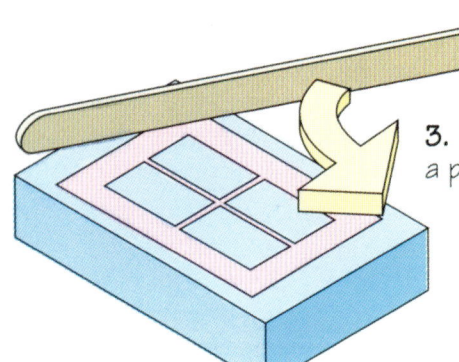

3. Skim any excess resin off with a popsicle stick or tongue depressor.

4. When the resin has cured, carefully peel back the mold to release the cast part. Now you can begin again.

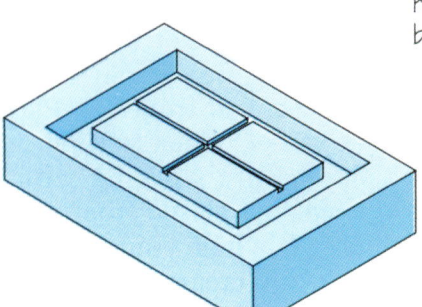 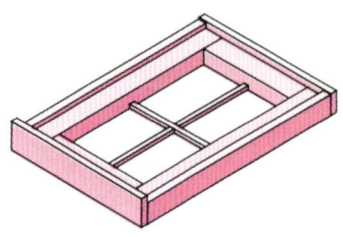

Casting in an RTV mold

them in the mold. You would have to tear the rubber to release the master.

Think of it like this: There will always be a flat side that will be the back side of the part. Don't worry if you make a mistake here, because what you must do to correct it will be obvious. If your master has some small spaces between it and the base, these can be filled with clay or wax. When making windows, it may be easier to build your original right on a base. This will eliminate the problem altogether.

After the part has been secured to the base and sealed, build a watertight "dam" around it. Depending on what the master is made of, it may be necessary to use a mold-release agent. Do not use a silicone-based mold release! The RTV rubber is silicone-based, and using a silicone mold release would have the opposite effect. Tap Plastics carries a special release agent for use in making molds. Usually, if the master is made of plastic, no release agent is needed. If wood or other porous material is used, a release agent is needed. You can usually use paste wax or Vaseline, but take care in application as they will blur detail if applied too heavily.

Molds can be made to build complete structures such as these logging camp skid shacks. In this case I made one mold to make the right and left ends, as well as one for the front wall and one for the back wall. The roofs are sheet styrene covered with wet/dry sandpaper to simulate particalized tar paper.

Mix the RTV rubber following the manufacturer's directions. The proper quantity to mix is learned by trial and error, unless you're a math whiz and can compute the required volume. I'm not, so I guess. However, since RTV is expensive, I try not to waste the material. It's a good idea to have an extra item or two to mold standing by so you can use any excess RTV in that mold. If you do not have enough leftover RTV to complete a standby mold, don't worry about it. Wrap the unfinished mold in plastic wrap to keep it clean, and the next time you mix RTV you can finish it. The rubber will bond to itself as long as the surface is clean.

When RTV is coated with a mold release such as Vaseline, it will not stick to itself. This will allow you to make two-part molds.

Mix the rubber and the catalyst together thoroughly, but do not over-agitate the mixture, as excessive air bubbles will form. Most manufacturers provide the catalyst in a color such as blue or red so you can see when it is thoroughly mixed. Complete mixing is very important; if pockets of un-catalyzed rubber end up near the molded surface, your mold will not solidify properly. For this reason, do not scrape the sides of the mixing pot when pouring.

If you have a vacuum chamber, the next step is to evacuate the air. If you don't own a vacuum chamber, here is a simple method for de-airing the rubber. Place the pot of mixed rubber in a bucket, then swing it around. This will force the rubber down and the air up to the surface. You will see dozens of tiny air bubbles come to the surface. While this does not work as well as a vacuum chamber, it is better than doing nothing.

Now pour the rubber into the mold and over the master. Do this slowly, starting at one corner. Be sure the rubber flows smoothly. Try to pour so the rubber rises slowly and completely surrounds the part. If you have any undercuts, run a piece of bent wire under the undercut to remove as much trapped air as possible. If the mold will fit into a bucket, you can swing it to remove trapped air. You can also tap the mold box on a table top to release trapped air. Do not put your uncured mold in the

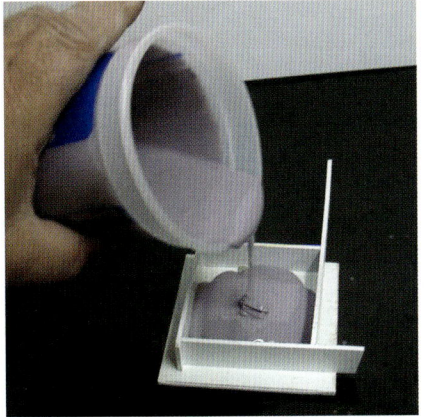

De-aired rubber is being poured into the mold box over the master.

After the rubber is poured, tap the mold box on a hard surface to help remove any trapped air. Set it on a level surface and let it cure.

On the left is the master. In the center is the mold made of the master, and on the right is the finished part.

vacuum chamber! Wait 24 hours for the rubber to cure.

To release the mold, remove the dam and carefully peel the rubber away from the base and the master. Sometimes the rubber will be tacky. If this is the case, sprinkle a little talcum powder on it. Do not try to release the mold if the rubber is not fully cured, as you could damage it. (Damaged or torn molds can often be repaired with silicone or RTV molding rubber.)

Making parts

You can use any one of several materials to make your castings. The one commonly used by model makers is polyurethane resin, a two-part product that is mixed 1:1. Polyurethane resin is not to be confused with clear casting resin or fiber glass resins that are catalyzed with just a few drops of catalyst. Other casting materials include low-melting-temperature metals and cement. I will limit my discussion here to polyurethane resin.

Mix the resin in disposable cups. A popsicle stick or tongue depressor makes an ideal mixing tool. Be sure that you do the mixing in a dry, well-ventilated area. Moisture will cause the material to bubble when curing, so mix it thoroughly but do not over-agitate. Resin can be messy; if it gets on your hands it is hard to get off. Wear gloves or use a glove-coat cream.

Resin cures quickly, so mix only as much as you can work during its "open" time, usually about a minute. At first the resin will flow freely like maple syrup, but it soon thickens and flows more like honey. At this point, it is starting to catalyze. When this happens you should stop pouring it, unless all the detail surfaces are already covered and you are filling for bulk only.

In some cases, you may need to use a popsicle stick to help the resin flow into all parts of the mold. If there is a hole for a doorknob, for example, use the stick to make sure the air is removed and the cavity is filled with resin.

The ideal material?

Over the years I have been searching for a suitable material from which to make outdoor structures, one that would last more than just a few years in the weather. Earlier in this book I discussed wood, plywood, Masonite, Styrofoam, and other materials, all of which can be made somewhat weatherproof. However, all will eventually break down or, in the case of Styrofoam, become somewhat fragile. I have found styrene, PVC, ABS, and resin relatively easy to work with and to be the most weather-resistant materials for outdoor structures. Styrene can be cut into just about any shape and can be easily and permanently bonded to itself. Polyurethane resin can be molded into any shape. Both can be finished to look like wood, metal, brick, stone, or just about anything else. When properly UV-protected by painting and when appropriately braced and bonded, these plastics form a strong weather-resistant structure. Refer to chapter 4 for details on how to join and reinforce resin parts.

Using these materials, I have developed my own building system. I create sheets of building materials. I made masters that simulate different types of building materials, including a clapboard wall measuring 10.5" x 14", a wood-shingled roof piece measuring 7" x 16", a rough-cut board wall or floor measuring 14" x 20", and an asphalt-shingled roof piece measuring 7.25" x 14". The average thickness of these sections is about ¼".

I made molds of these walls and roofs following the methods described earlier. (See page 71.) When I want to make a clapboard building, I just cast the appropriate number of wall pieces to make it. Since the clapboard is a one-piece casting instead of individual boards, it will never delaminate or come apart in the weather. The same is true if I want to put a wood-shingled roof on a building—I just cast enough roof material to do the job. Since the shingles are part of a one-piece casting, they will never fall off.

The dimensions mentioned above are what I chose for my sheets of material, but they could be any size you like. I like these sizes because they are either the average size of a roof panel or, in the case of the clapboard sheet, the right size for a two-story structure. In the case of the rough board, I can get pieces of several different sizes and shapes from one sheet.

Once cured, polyurethane resin has the working characteristics of particle board or plywood. It can be cut, sanded, and shaped. I cut the material to the exact size I need. Then, in the case of a wall, I cut the door and window openings out just as I would with plywood.

The Dutch colonial house at left and the impressive Georgian mansion at right were both built entirely out of resin (except for Grandt Line doors and windows) with the sheet material discussed above.

◀ Fog Harbor is almost entirely composed of resin buildings. The only negative effects from weather that I have seen with resin buildings are the paint breaking down and some warping if the buildings are not properly braced with wood in the corners and along the seams or edges.

Notice the de-lamination that has taken place on this resin part. The reason this occurred is it was poured in two layers. This should be avoided. Cured resin does not bond well to new resin. In cases where you must pour new resin over cured resin (as when adding resin as corner reinforcement), it is important to rough up the cured resin to remove the parting agent and to create some tooth to improve bonding with the new resin.

Again, once you have a few different molds made, keep an extra close by and pour any leftover resin into the second mold, so you don't waste any product.

As with making the molds, trapped air bubbles can ruin a part when casting. In simple, open-pour molds, running a popsicle stick over and into the tight areas is usually enough to release trapped air. In some cases, as with more complex shapes, it may be necessary to use other methods. One such method is the "swinging bucket," discussed earlier.

Most manufacturers state that you do not need a mold release when using RTV rubber molds and polyurethane resin. This is generally true, but I have found that in time, the mold breaks down without a mold release agent. The resin eventually seeps into the surface of the rubber and will start pulling off bits of rubber when the part is removed, ruining the mold. I use spray paint as a mold release. Aside from making it easier to pull the parts, it will prolong the mold life. It also provides a pre-primed part.

Not all molds can be painted inside. If this is the case, all parts must be thoroughly washed before they are painted to remove the mold-release agent that is in the resin. Liquid dishwashing detergent works well.

Knowing how to make a mold and using polyurethane resin as a building material opens up a whole new level of outdoor model making. This material may have conquered the weather problem. Only time will tell, of course, but I expect my resin structures to be around for many years to come.

SOURCES

Alumilite
315 E. North St.
Kalamazoo, MI 49007
800-447-9344
www.alumilite.com
Mold-making and casting products. Their web site has good tutorials and videos demonstrating their products.

Douglas & Sturgess, Inc.
730 Bryant St.
San Francisco, CA 94107
415-896-6283
Sculpture tools, materials, and supplies. Catalog: $5

Circle K Products
47825 DeLuz Rd.
Temecula, CA 92590-4308
951-695-1955
Manufacturer of RTV silicone mold-making rubber.

Dow Corning Corporation
P.O. Box 994
Midland, MI 48686-0994
989-496-4400
dowcorning.com
Manufacturer of RTV silicone mold-making rubber.

Silpak
470 E. Bonita Ave.
Pomona, CA 91767
909-625-0056
www.silpak.com
Manufacturer and sellers of RTV rubber "R-1104 A & B," casting material "Silwhite" plastic, mold release for masters "MR-1500," mold release for parts "ER-2300."

Tap Plastics, Inc.
6475 Sierra Lane
Dublin, CA 94568
510-828-7744
Retail dealer, supplier of "Quick Cast" and all types of plastic

Making a vacuum chamber

Air bubbles are the No. 1 enemy in mold making as well as in casting. If a small air bubble forms near the molded surface, that bubble can break in time, at best causing a ball to form on your part or worse, tearing and ruining your mold. A vacuum chamber is a vessel in which the mixed rubber is placed (before it sets) and the air bubbles are evacuated by means of a vacuum pump.

According to manufacturers, the rubbers discussed here are formulated to release air bubbles without a vacuum, but you still could have problems with air bubbles. If you plan to make a lot of molds, buy or make a vacuum chamber. The vacuum pump should be able to pull 29" of mercury. A simple vacuum chamber can be homemade from inexpensive hardware-store items.

I used a 6"-diameter PVC pipe joint and an 8" x 8" x ¼" sheet of clear acrylic to make the top portion of the chamber. I glued the acrylic to one end of the pipe joint and sealed it with silicone. For the base plate, I laminated a flat piece of rubber to a piece of plywood. This unit is large enough to enclose a 16-ounce pot of RTV.

Set the pot of RTV on the rubber-padded base plate, then place the vacuum chamber over the pot, making sure it contacts the rubber all around its circumference. Start the vacuum pump. A vacuum pump and fittings can be obtained from a local pump dealer. Check the yellow pages under "pumps" or "vacuum." Your local dealer can help you select the right pump and fittings if you tell him how large your chamber is, and that you want to pump 29" of mercury. The fitting for the chamber is inserted into a hole drilled in the base plate, then mounted using a nut and washer. The fitting is sealed with silicone.

Once a you have created a vacuum, the rubber keeps the seal airtight. Keep the RTV in the chamber until the air has completely evacuated, about four or five minutes. The rubber

This is the author's homemade vacuum chamber, made from a PVC pipe coupling and ½" clear acrylic. The valve is where the vacuum hose is connected. The vacuum draws through the fitting unimpeded and the valve has no effect on the flow. The valve is actually on a "T." When the valve is open, it allows the vacuum to be relieved.

will appear to boil as the air is removed. To remove the pot, open the bleed screw, let the chamber return to normal atmospheric pressure, then remove the top.

It is easy to check for leaks. Pump out the air and listen for hissing. If you locate a leak, apply silicone to it from the atmosphere side. The vacuum will pull the silicone into the leak. Release the vacuum once the seal has been made to allow the silicone to cure fully.

The fittings used on the unit in the picture are designed to bleed off the vacuum without having to remove the hose, so the pump and chamber are always hooked up.

The vacuum chamber has been placed over the pot with the RTV rubber in it. The valve is closed, then the chamber is de-aired with the vacuum pump.

Here's the rubber in the chamber while being de-aired. It appears to be boiling as the air removed.

The rubber looks like this after being de-aired. The bubbles you see are at the surface and will soon disappear.

Textured walls and roofs

CHAPTER 12

Texture is an important part of the overall look and feel of a miniature structure. There are many methods you can employ to add texture to a smooth surface.

San Mateo, on the author's layout, is on a hillside, but you still look down on it. A variety of roof shapes adds interest.

Stucco finish

Stucco is a common way to finish a building in the full-size world. To create a stucco look on an otherwise smooth surface like Masonite or plywood, mix very fine sand (I use Woodland Scenic's HO scale railroad ballast) into exterior-grade latex paint, and apply it with a brush. Add about three or four teaspoons of sand for each half cup of paint. This mixture creates a rough, sandy surface that looks just like stucco. Don't paint the trim of your buildings with this mixture, though, because wood trim should remain smooth.

A word of caution: You can buy texture kits at dollhouse shops, but this material is usually not intended for outdoor use. I tried such a product on one of my dollhouse kits and it peeled off over time. Brick- and stone-texture kits are also available. They too are intended for indoor structures and should not be used outdoors. I discuss stone and brick textures for outdoor use in another chapter.

Stipple paint, which is used on drywall to give a rough texture, is another product that can be used for simulating stucco. Stipple paint is normally rolled on with a roller that makes the rough texture. While you may be able to use a small roller for parts of your structure, you will not be able to get into tight spots. Instead of a roller, use a stiff-bristle brush (similar to a stenciling brush or an acid brush) to create the texture. Use dabbing strokes to raise the paint.

For a finer finish, Rust-Oleum Sand Stone spray can texturing paint gives a nice sandy texture, and it is available in several colors.

Adobe finish

A finished adobe building has a texture similar to that of stucco, but is not as sandy or rough looking.

To achieve the desired texture, you will need to make special tools. You'll need a miniature trowel, which can be made from scrap sheet metal or from brass stock obtained from a hobby shop. You don't have to worry about making it to scale, but it should be the same shape as a full-size trowel. (See "Miniature garden tools for your work crew," by C.R. Garbett, *Garden Railways,* June 1994, for fabrication instructions).

Using the miniature trowel, apply texture using paintable silicone. Create swirls with a brush, or a use sponge for finer texture. Practice on a scrap piece of board first. Keep your tools wet with water, so you can spread, smooth, and tease your texture into the form you want. Just have fun and see what you can create.

An interesting thing happens using this method. The walls may develop hairline cracks, which actually look pretty realistic. The paint and the silicone expand and contract at different rates, creating cracks in the paint.

The stucco on Father Leo's church was patterned after San Francisco's Mission Delores. The Masonite shell was first painted with house paint, then a coat of stucco was heavily applied.

If you don't want the cracks in your work, you can use other materials like Fix-All patching compound or hydraulic or patching cement. Fix-All is not waterproof, but it will withstand the elements with a coat of paint. The cement products are weatherproof.

Heavy texturing can be accomplished using plastic automotive-body filler such as Bondo. Plastic filler can be mixed and spread over plastic, and a texture can be added using a tool to gouge out the material. A finer-grain version, called glazing putty, works well for detail work.

Plastic filler has solvent in it so it adheres well to plastic. Plastic body

Miniature trowels to work stucco

A variety of stucco patterns can be modeled with a miniature trowel, brush, or sponge.

fillers can be thinned by adding polyester resin. Mix the un-catalyzed resin and plastic filler together to the consistency that works for you. After mixing thoroughly, add the catalyst. (The amount of catalyst is usually a percentage of the mass. This information is on the product label. When catalyzing the mixed material, calculate your catalyst based on the entire mass of the plastic body filler and polyester resin.)

Magic Sculp is another material that creates texture (see chapter 10).

Brick

Brick is a common material used to build structures. Houseworks makes ½" scale brickwork in sheets and corners. It forms a nice clean wall and corner joint. Doors and windows have to be cut out, and window and door castings (such as Grandt Line) must be used. (There is no easy way to reproduce arched windows and doors with this product.)

Good brickwork can be difficult to replicate accurately with ready-made materials. Styrofoam or Precision Board can be used to simulate brick (see chapter 9 for details on these materials).

I use a laser cutter to make bricks. This allows me to accurately reproduce the exact pattern of the original.

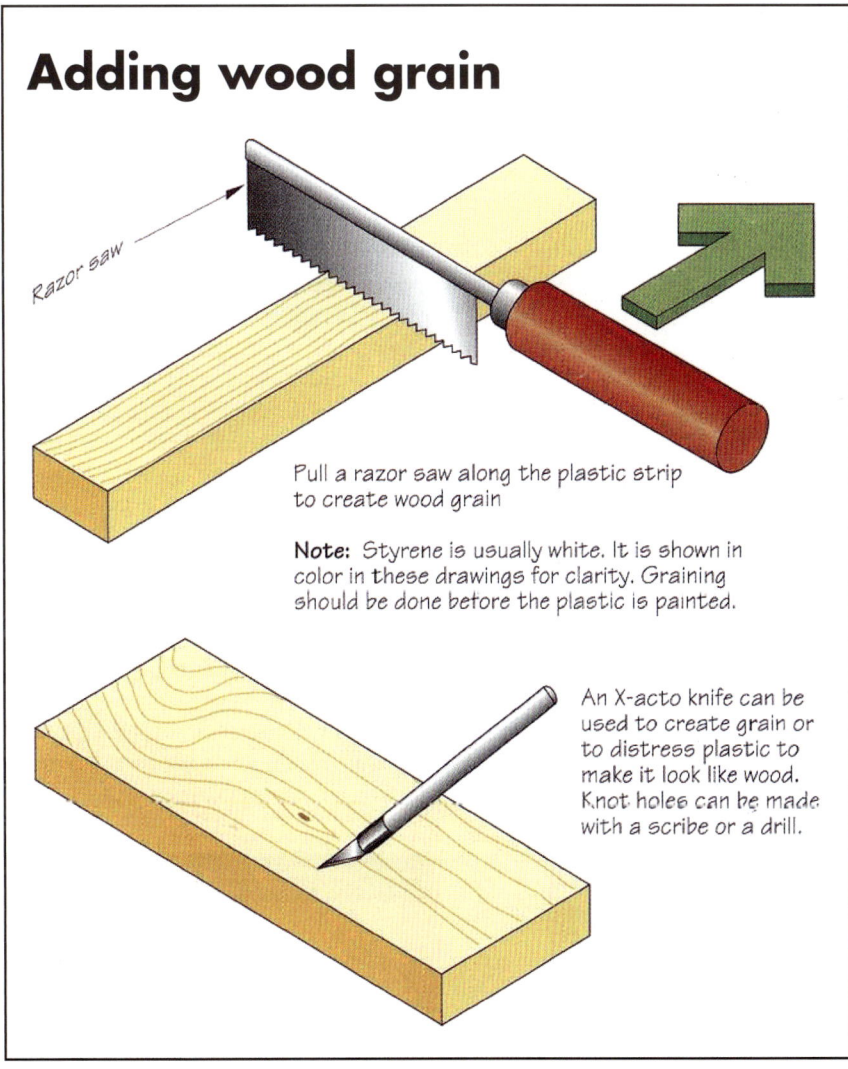

Adding wood grain

Pull a razor saw along the plastic strip to create wood grain

Note: Styrene is usually white. It is shown in color in these drawings for clarity. Graining should be done before the plastic is painted.

An X-acto knife can be used to create grain or to distress plastic to make it look like wood. Knot holes can be made with a scribe or a drill.

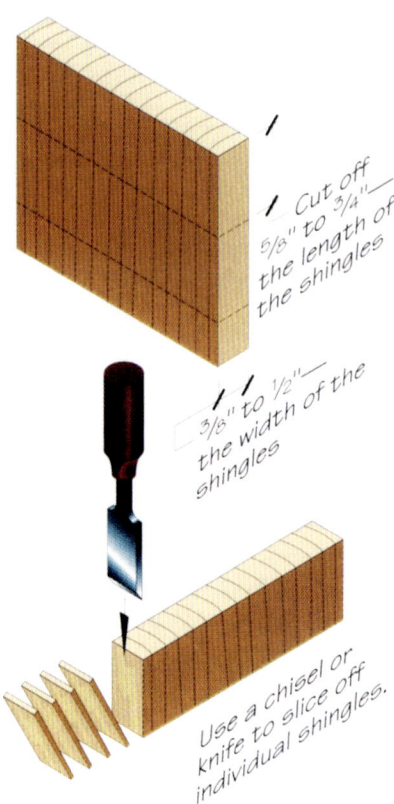

Figure 2

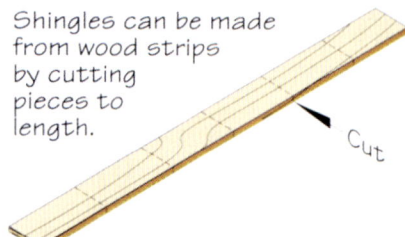

Figure 1

Bricks can also be cut out of styrene plastic and glued to a base sheet. A finished sheet can be used as a master, allowing you to duplicate the parts.

Roofs

Roofing and roof designs are especially important on garden railroad buildings since, just like a real roof, they protect your structures from the elements. In most cases, we are looking down at our buildings, so we constantly look at the roofs. This means they are a high visibility item, more so than in real life. Vary your roof colors and types to make them more interesting to look at. I try to include a number of flat roofs, peaked roofs or various pitches and dormers in my buildings to add some interest. Let's look at a few methods you can use for roofing your buildings.

Particalized tar paper

This tar paper has small particles of rock imbedded in it. It is one of the easier roofing materials to duplicate in miniature. I use wet/dry sandpaper. The grit depends on the scale. I use 120 grit for 1:24 models. I cut the sheets into strips about 1½" wide to simulate tar paper from a 3' wide full-size tar paper roll. In practice, the material is applied either horizontally or vertically. I use silicone to hold the material in place. This is the roof that was installed on the author's roundhouse (shown in chapter 6).

Another common roofing material is asphalt shingles. I also simulate these with wet-dry sandpaper. I use my laser cutter to cut these in to shape, but a band saw also works well. When using a band saw, stack up the sandpaper and cut through multiple layers simultaneously. The stacked material is easier to handle than individual strips. Use masking tape to bundle the sheets of sandpaper together. See the cutting pattern. I prefer to adhere shingles with tape adhesive, such as Killer Red. I apply the first side of the adhesive to the sandpaper before cutting. This is the roof used on the cottage built in chapter 6.

Make your own wood shingles

Shingles can be made by cutting cedar, redwood, or other suitable woods into thin strips. Cut the wood to the thickness and width of a scale shingle. Then cut off pieces the lengthwise (see **fig. 1**). Full-size shingles vary in size, depending on where they were milled and their style.

Another method of making shingles is to split them like real shakes. Find or cut a board about ⅜" to ½" thick, the width of the shingle. Cut off a section about ⅝" to ¾" wide, the length of the shingle. The resulting piece of wood is ready to be split into shingles one by one using a chisel or knife.

This method provides great-looking shingles. Since they are split like full-size shingles, they will have the proper texture and the grain will run in the correct direction (see **fig. 2**). If you intend to stain or paint your shingles, it is best to do this prior to applying them to the roof.

Shingling the roof. Time to install the shingles! A sub-roof can be made from Masonite or other similar material. Draw horizontal lines on the sub-roof approximately ½" apart. These serve as guides to help keep the rows straight. Apply the shingles from the bottom upward. Begin in the lower left corner, and work to the right and upward.

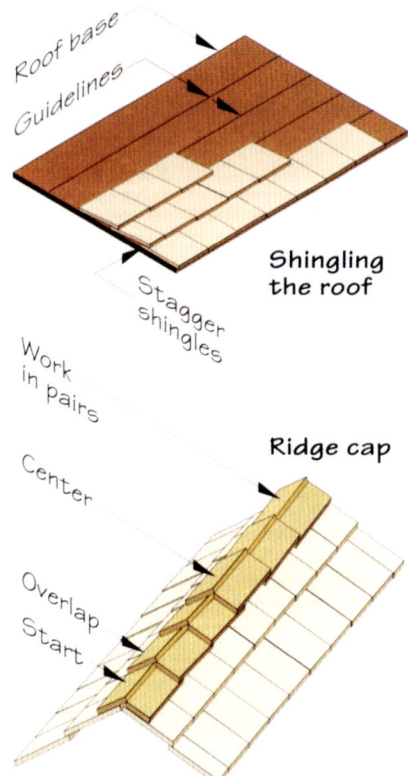

Figure 3

Pattern for shingles made out of 180-grit wet/dry sandpaper. Stagger and apply them one over the other.

Apply silicone to the sub-roof. Work in small areas, because the silicone cures quickly.

I use the tip of a No. 11 blade in a hobby knife to pick up each shingle by poking it with the knife point. Place the shingle in the proper position. You will be able to move the piece for alignment purposes for about 10 minutes before the silicone cures. Lay down three or four rows, then align them with a metal straightedge. Place the straightedge along the bottom edge of a row and gently align the shingles. Use the knife to pull individual shingles into position. Sometimes an entire row will need to be moved up, which can be done easily with the straightedge. You must work quickly! When the silicone cures, the shingles will be immovable.

Shingles, when laid out, should overlap the row below and should be staggered from right to left so that the edges are offset. This means that every other row will start with a half-width shingle and the other with a full-width shingle (**fig. 3**). A pair of garden scissors can be used to cut the shingles at angles for fitting into odd areas.

The corrugated metal roof for the author's saw mill was made from aluminum stock formed in a die like the one shown on page 83. A rack-and-pinion type press was used to apply pressure. The sheets were painted gray on the inside and weathered rust on the outside.

Be sure to press each shingle into the wet silicone to form a tight bond. Leave a small gap between shingles to allow for swelling when they get wet. Try to keep excess silicone from getting on the shingles. If some does go astray, wait until it has cured, then peel or cut off the excess. A word of caution: Do not use white glue or hot glue on roofs intended for outdoor use, because the bond won't last.

If you have a complex roof design, such as a dormer roof, flashing may be necessary to cover the joint. Flashing can be made from aluminum-colored duct tape. Cut the tape into ½"-wide strips, then lay it over the joint. Do not depend on the tape's adhesive alone to adhere it: smear silicone over the tape to seal and bond it.

When the shingles have reached the peak of the roof and the last row has been completed, it's time to make a ridge cap. First, lay a row of shingles horizontally along each side of the peak of the roof. A shingle on one side should be lined up with its counterpart on the other, almost as if they were one piece. In fact, the best way to do this is in pairs. Front and rear ridge-shingles should be paired up, then each pair of shingles should overlap the last.

Start at one end of the ridge and lay down the first pair. The next pair should overlap the first pair, and so on. Work to the center of the ridge line and stop. Then, start at the opposite end and work toward the center. Cover the point where the two halves of the row meet with a pair of shingles that

The South Pass Bar is a cast-resin structure, but it has a real corrugated-metal roof. This roof was made with a die like the one in the drawing on the next page. The panels were made from very thin aluminum stock.

overlap the ends of both halves (**fig. 3**). If this seems complicated, look at a full-size wood-shingled roof before you begin.

An alternate method of applying shingles one at a time is this: Line up the shingles along a straightedge on your work table, then lay a piece of masking tape over the row. You can then pick up the entire row at once and lay it on the roof.

Corrugated-metal roofs

Metal was, and still is, a popular roofing material, especially on commercial structures. I make my own corrugated roofing with a small homemade die. I use very thin aluminum sheet that is cut to size (2" x 4" is 4' x 8' in 1:24 scale). Pieces are placed in the die and pressed into shape. Miniature corrugated metal is also available commercially.

You can buy commercial metal roofing material made from real metal from Rainbow Ridge, or buy plastic sheets of simulated corrugated metal from Plastruct.

Generally speaking, when making an iron roof you should make a sub-roof of plywood, Masonite, plastic, or similar material. Use silicone to glue the metal sheets to the sub-roof. If you're making a structure with an interior, or if you wish to see the underside of the roof, attach the metal to a wood frame, which is how full-size iron roofs are made. In looking through prototypical ghost-town books, many photos show metal roofs with pieces half-attached, revealing the wood framing below. This would be an interesting effect for depicting old, abandoned buildings.

One problem with aluminum is its shininess. If you are making a modern building with real aluminum roofing, this is OK. But if you are modeling an older structure that would have been made out of iron or galvanized metal, the aluminum should be toned down. Paint the roof with at least one coat of flat gray paint if you want the appearance of a new roof, or use Floquil Roof Brown paint to give the material a rusty look. Weathering chalks can add highlights and shadows.

Make your own corrugated metal material

If you are good at soldering and metalworking, you can build your own die for making corrugated metal from thin aluminum sheets. If you do not want to tackle this, you can make an even simpler die that will make corrugated metal out of heavy-duty aluminum foil.

Heavy-duty die. For this tool you will need 80" of 1/16"-diameter brass rod and a 4" x 5" sheet of 1/16"-thick brass. From the brass, cut two 2" x 4" pieces. Then cut 20 pieces of rod, each 4" long. The two sheets of brass will become the two halves of the die. Lay the brass rods lengthwise on the brass sheets, spaced at about 3/16" center to center. Lay out the rods on each sheet so they will interlock with the mating side.

Solder the rods to the brass sheets. At this point, you will have an interlocking die. Fasten the halves of the metal die to blocks of hardwood or metal, adding some guides to make the die usable. Glue one side of the die to a 2" x 4" block, then fasten pieces of wood or metal to three sides of the block to act as guides (see drawings). Glue the other half of the die to another block of hardwood or metal, this time without guides.

To use this die, cut several 2" x 4" pieces of aluminum shim stock. If you need shorter pieces, cut the shim to size before forming them. (If you cut them to length after forming, you will flatten the corrugation.) Insert the aluminum into the die, then press until the metal is formed. There are several methods of applying pressure. Depending on how thick the metal is, more or less pressure may be necessary. If you use aluminum foil, hand pressure will be enough. If you use heavier material, you may need a mechanical device, such as a vise. A screw or hydraulic press could also be used, or you could strike the die with a rubber mallet.

The simple method. This die will make corrugated metal out of heavy-duty aluminum foil. You will need a piece of corrugated-rubber rug runner. This can be bought by the foot from a hardware or home-products store. Cut a strip to fit a curved sanding block and install it in the block, corrugated side out.

Cut aluminum foil sheets 2¼" x 4", or to whatever size you need. Lay the foil over another piece of corrugated rubber. Match the corrugations in the rubber so they interlock, then roll the sanding pad over the aluminum foil. When doing this, do not press too hard. Excessive pressure using any of the methods discussed here will tear the foil. Experiment a little to determine what's best.

An even simpler method. You can make corrugated metal from aluminum foil by placing a piece of foil over a piece of rubber rug runner (as used above) and simply rub your fingers over it. This method is slow, but it does work.

Using the same basic methods described above, other dies could be made to resemble modern metal siding, like those used on Butler buildings. There are a variety of patterns to choose from. One that can be done easily is an alternating high and low pattern, where the panel is raised for 6" and then recessed for 6" (see the drawing to the right). Almost any pattern can be made once you know how to make a die. Just think, the next time an aluminum-siding salesman calls, you can tell him, "No thanks, I make my own."

Other types of metal siding

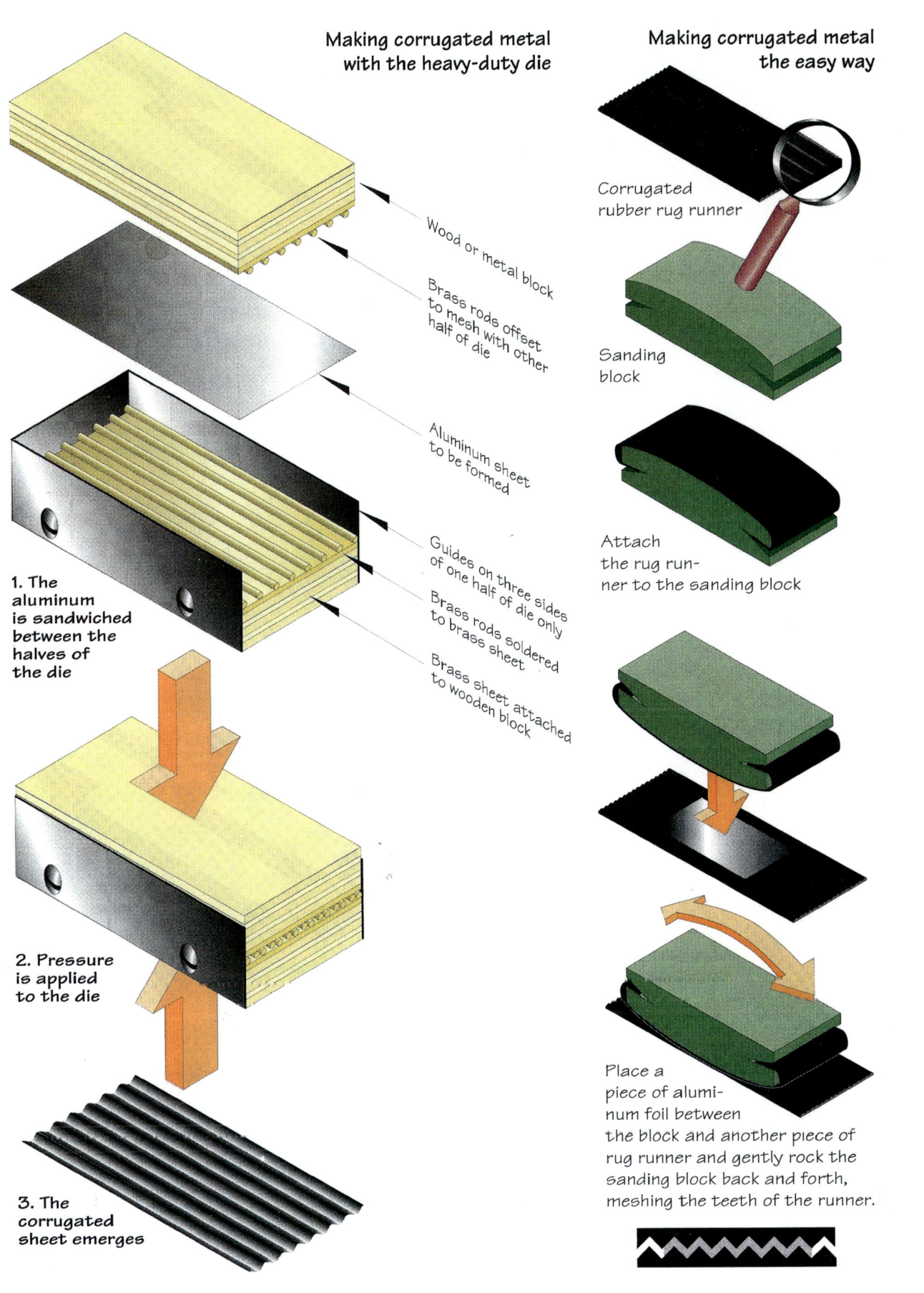

CHAPTER 13

Painting for protection and finish

A coat of paint can not only create a fresh new, colorful appearance, with time and exposure, it can also give you a naturally aged look as here on the author's stamp mill. Paint also provides the UV protection some materials, such as resin, need to last a long time in your garden railway.

Unless you are working in wood and you want your structure to weather naturally, you will need to give it a coat of paint to protect it from the elements. Paint helps protect plastic surfaces from harmful ultraviolet rays from the sun, and is a must on cast-resin buildings for both appearance and protection.

Primer

Primer is an important step in the preservation of your model. I use one of two basic approaches, one for wood and wood products, such as Masonite and plywood and Styrofoam, and another for plastics. For the former, I use a heavy primer, such as latex house paint. The paint has "body" and forms a heavy coat of protection. It seals wood and does not attack Styrofoam. Because it's heavier and thicker than model paint, however, it's difficult not to leave brush marks. You can turn this to your favor by deliberately making your brush stroke to resemble wood grain, or create a stipple finish for simulated stucco or adobe.

I use spray-on primer for plastic. Years ago, I used an air brush to apply primer. An airbrush gives you more control than a spray can, but I've found that aerosol cans work just fine on large-scale models. Spray cans are easy to use, and you don't have to clean them like you do an airbrush. Spray primer applies smoothly and evenly, dries quickly, and is sandable. My favorite primer is Kryon brand sandable primer, available in white, ruddy brown, flat black and gray. I still use an airbrush for special effects, as I'll explain in a bit.

A simple paint job will protect resin and plastic models from ultraviolet light. Here, Krylon white primer and American Accents seaside green were sprayed from cans.

Wood

Wood is a material that can be either painted or left natural. If you'd like your buildings to weather naturally, leave the wood bare. Soft, white woods like bass wood and pine do not fare well when left bare, however. They will rot away in anywhere from one year to a couple of years, depending on the conditions. Woods like redwood, cedar, walnut, and mahogany will last much longer than soft white woods.

All woods will eventually turn gray and eventually rot away when left untreated. It is a matter of choosing the wood that will last the longest. I don't use wood sealers; they slow down the weathering process, and they really

With only a few exceptions, all of these buildings were painted with spray cans. Some of them have trim and other details that were brush-painted with acrylic paints.

The roundhouse was originally painted with a ruddy brown primer. I wanted this building to weather naturally, so I applied the spray primer directly on the redwood. Due to its natural oils, redwood needs a special primer to hold paint and to prevent bleed through. By skipping this step, though, the paint eventually peeled, giving me the weathered look I wanted.

This view shows natural weathering and detailing. This is a resin structure that was spray painted and detailed with acrylic paint. What I like about this scene is how nature is trying to reclaim the area: The building is weathering naturally, the dirt is working its way into the seams, and the moss is growing up around the tracks.

for model-size boards used for planking and trim. Rougher grades work well for wooden trestles, tunnel portals, retaining walls, and bracing.

You can speed up the weathering process on redwood with the application of a simple liquid. Add a tablespoon of baking soda to a quart of water. Paint or dip the redwood with this mixture. This will turn the redwood gray immediately. Some of the color will wash off in the weather, but this liquid does speed up the natural aging process. If you use this method, be sure the wood has dried thoroughly before you glue it.

I used redwood for my log dump at the mill pond. Two-thirds of the structure is under water, and amazingly the redwood lasted over 10 years before it had to be replaced. Note: if you plan to paint the wood, you don't have to use redwood. In fact, painting redwood has its own problems. The natural elements in the wood tend to bleed through, and you'll need to apply a special primer.

The best paint for wood is ordinary latex house paint. I buy the best quality "mistake" paint I can find. Most hardware or paint stores have paint available that was mixed and later returned because the color wasn't just right. Often, these cans of paint are sold at an incredible discount. There is nothing wrong with the paint; it is just the "wrong" color. Fortunately, as a primer, paint color isn't an issue.

When painting wood, paint all sides and edges to keep out the elements. Once you have a good coat of latex paint down, use almost any other type of paint to add color(s). Model paints, such as Floquil, will apply easily over latex paint. Floquil on its own is not robust enough to last over bare wood much longer that a couple of months, but when applied onto a latex painted surface, it will last a long time. The same is true for acrylic paints. Acrylic by itself will last for a long time, but this time can be extended by using latex as an undercoat.

Plastic and resin buildings

Although Floquil and acrylic paints can be applied directly to plastics, I still apply a primer coat first. On plastic, primer adds an additional barrier of

don't work that well. If you are going to stain, paint, or glue wood, do not apply water sealer. This prevents penetration or these materials.

I like redwood for the projects I leave bare. You can buy redwood in the form of fence boards, which are relatively inexpensive. Pick and choose the best boards. You want boards with few knots, the straightest and tightest grain, and the least amount of warp. You also want the best-seasoned wood. The older the wood, the more red it is. Young redwood is not red; it light beige.

Redwood is also available as kiln-dried heartwood. This is the best grade

protection, and gives you a better painting surface. Primer will give the surface "tooth," which enables paints to bond better to the surface than unpainted plastic or resins. Two popular brands of primers that work well on plastic are Krylon and Rust-Oleum.

Once your project has a coat of primer, add the finish. In some cases, the primer itself can serve as the finish.

There are large number of colors available in spray cans that are perfect for painting structures. I like to use spray can paint for my base color. Then I'll use model or crafts paints to do the trim. I use a brush to paint the trim colors.

Trim colors

Acrylic paints are ideal for painting trim on model structures. There are hundreds of colors available from a number of manufacturers, available in bottles from 3 ounces up to 16 ounces. Common brands include Americana, Cracker Barrel, Delta, and Folk Art. Acrylic paint can be thinned with water, and it can be used in airbrushes. It goes on smooth and cleans up easily with water.

A number of model railroad paints are available such as Floquil, Testor's, and Scalecoat. Floquil manufactures a large number of colors. Many colors are for a specific railroad's rolling stock, but they also offer colors for structures. Floquil paint goes on smooth and dries to a matte finish.

Most types of model paints can be used to paint plastic. Check the label to be sure the paint will not harm the plastic. If you are going to brush on a lacquer-base paint, it may be necessary to apply a barrier coat first, since lacquer could eat the plastic. Usually, this is not a problem if the lacquer is sprayed on and not allowed to puddle. In any case, you should test your paint of choice on a piece of scrap plastic before using it on your project.

Finish

For indoor models, three types of finishes are available: matte, flat, and gloss. Most modelers prefer a matte or flat finish. Generally, a glossy finish does not look right when viewing or photographing miniatures. The shine looks out of place or out of scale. Even an object like an automobile that is glossy in real life looks toy like in miniature when it is too shiny.

When you look at a model, it's similar to seeing the full-size item from a distance. You don't see things as vividly from a distance, so scale model colors are usually muted and matte finished. In a garden railroad, this is not as big a factor as it is indoors. The observer is usually 10 feet away from the model; especially when the garden railway is built on the ground.

Even shiny buildings will eventually develop a dull finish as they weather from the effects of the elements. If you like, you could simply put your struc-

Fog Harbor is shown here from the working side. The freight house roof is cast resin in the form of corrugated metal. It is finished with ruddy brown primer and Bragdon weathering powders were brushed into the paint to produce a rusty look.

tures outside and let them weather naturally.

I like to use matte or flat paints. This gives me the finish I want right away. When the building starts to weather on its own, it is further enhanced by nature. If you bring your buildings inside and want them weathered, you will have to add the weathering.

Weathering

Weathering is the art of taking a new scale model and making it look like it has been outdoors. I use the word art because weathering is not an exact science, and you need an artful eye to do it well. It is better to be subtle. Heavy weathering requires more skill to keep your model from looking garish.

Even if you choose to let your structures weather naturally, there are certain elements that you will need to weather yourself. If you made a smoke jack, simulated iron hinges, or other simulated metal parts out of plastic they will never rust in nature. In this case, you will have to add the rust. The same holds true for a metal roof made out of aluminum foil or cans. This roof would never rust, so you'd need to create the rust.

There are several methods that you can use to weather a model. Certain techniques work better on certain things; there is no one way to do everything. Feel free to experiment. Sometimes I'll combine techniques to come up with something different.

Airbrush

An airbrush can be used in several ways. One way is as miniature spray gun, for when you want to apply paint over a large area.

When using an airbrush as a spray gun, you want one with a large paint reservoir. Some airbrushes have a wide range of settings, allowing you to do anything from area painting to pin-striping with one nozzle. Others require you to change nozzles in order to change the pattern.

An airbrush allows you to apply any color you want. You are not limited to what is available in a spray can. The process involves mixing up the weathering color, then applying it. Use several colors to create the effect you want. First, apply a thin fogging of your basic color. Add various shades of weathering to achieve a blend of colors that looks natural. For example, you can spray on a light rust color for your base, then apply a light coat of grimy black to simulate coal dust or grime. Using an airbrush takes practice; this is best done on scraps to develop your technique.

Weathering with powders

Weathering can also be done with a variety of powders such as pastel artist's chalks, special weathering powders from companies like Bragdon Enterprises, dry concrete colors, and even real dirt.

Applying powders is fairly easy to learn; it's a forgiving technique for beginners. Most powders can be manipulated or even washed off and reapplied if you are not happy with the result. Powders don't stick thoroughly until you set or seal them.

Powders will not stick to glossy finishes. If you painted your structure with a primer or flat paint, you won't have a problem using this technique. If this is not the case, there are several ways to remedy this. One way is to use water to spread and hold the powders in place while you apply them. (Note: Water alone will not work to give you your final set. This will have to be done in another step.) The advantage of working with water is you can easily wash away the powders if you are not happy with the results.

Once you have applied the powders to your liking, lock them in place. One option is to spray the project with Krylon's workable fix. This product will lock the powders in place, but will allow you to work in additional layers. You can also spray on a clear matte finish or clear UV coating. You might lose a little of the subtle texture and shading, but you can re-apply powders over the finish to get a little of that back.

Another method is to spray your project with workable fix or a clear matte prior to applying the powders. This gives the powder something to stick to. The drawback is that even though you can remove some of the powder, you can't remove it all if you not happy with it. You can fix it in place using the same methods as above, or spray the work with a light coat of lacquer thinner. This fixes the color with the minimal amount of change to the texture and color.

Finally, an untraditional method of setting powders is to use zip kicker, a product used to set CA glue quickly. The zip kicker softens the surface enough to allow the powders to penetrate and stick. Spray your work surface with zip kicker, then apply powder colors.

These logging camp houses are resin kits from Big Train Backshop. I painted them with gray primer, then brushed on a thin wash of India ink thinned with alcohol to bring out the details and instantly weather the building.

Here are some basic paints that can be used for outdoor structures. In the back row left to right, OSH brand primer is shown, but Krylon and Rust-Oleum also make primers. Primer is available in gray, white, flat black, red, or ruddy brown. American Accents offers a wide variety of colors. These are matte finish and several match classic house colors. Rust-Oleum offers a number of textured paints, which are good choices for adding texture to smooth surfaces such as acrylic or styrene plastic. Krylon workable fix is used to work in powdered colors. Matte finish is a clear coat that does not shine and dull down gloss paints. UV-resistant clear is a protective coat that can be applied over paint or decals. In the front row left to right are some water-based acrylic craft paints that are available in hundreds of colors: Americana, Apple Barrel, DecoArt, Delta Ceramcoat, and Folk Art Acrylic.

Creating an old paint finish

I have always been fascinated by old structures that have stood up to years of weathering and that are barely standing. Many times the structure has none of the original paint left, but sometimes you can still see the faint remains of the original paint job.

Create this effect with powdered colors. Start with a gray primer. Most wood turns gray with age, so this makes a good base color. If your project has wood grain carved in, apply a little black or dark gray first to accent the grain. Work the black/gray into the grain, then remove the excess. Next, apply powdered color, mixing the powder with water as you brush it in.

Over time, wood can turn various colors depending on the climate. In photos of old buildings in the San Juan Mountains of Colorado and in Bodie, Calif., I noticed that the old wood turned an interesting shade of bright brown. To achieve this look on plastic, you can use stains. Stains are translucent, allowing a base color to come through. While you can buy commercial stains, try making your own using powdered colors or thinned paint and a carrier such as alcohol, water, or clear coat. Apply your stain in thin, translucent coats, creating layers of colors.

I find that oil-based stains go on better than water-based stains. Water-based stains work more like paint, in that they form an impenetrable barrier, preventing you from working colors deep into the surface.

Weathering with acrylic paint

Once you have painted your structure with a base color and it has dried thoroughly, you can weather your structure with an acrylic wash.

The process is simple. Thin acrylic paint with water, and use these washes to create water stains, streaks, and subtle color variations. A thin wash of charcoal or gray can be worked into cracks and crevices to enhance them.

Peeling paint

First, paint your structure a base color, such as a weathered gray to simulate old wood, a brown wood color, or a color to represent a previous paint job. Streak some rubber cement randomly over the structure and let it dry. Paint the entire structure with the color that will represent the latest paint job. Let the paint dry.

Go back to the areas coated with rubber cement and rub it off with an eraser. Once the rubber cement comes off, the base color of your structure will show through, simulating cracked or peeling paint.

SOURCES

Big Train Backshop
2437 Cumber Court S 41
San Luis Obispo, CA 93401
805-541-0546

Bragdon Enterprises
2960 Garden Tower Lane
Georgetown, CA 95634
530-333-1365
www.bragdonent.com

CHAPTER 14

As the town of San Mateo shows, a hillside makes an interesting setting. Structures are built along the side of a winding road that makes its way to the top of the hill. These structures are built on foundations made from concrete stepping stones. The exposed sides have been textured using Magic Sculp to simulate large stones.

Landscaping with model structures

Structures should be placed in your railroad with the same thought and care you've invested in the rest of your railroad. It makes no sense to spend hours building and detailing model structures, only to just set them on the ground.

I attended a garden-railroad event some time ago, and on the cover of the program was a photo showing a beautiful building with surrounding details. I put that railroad on my list of garden railroads to see. After arriving at the railroad, to my disappointment, I saw what did not show up in the picture. The structures were not leveled and were displayed in unnatural settings. The structures themselves where nicely done. If the builder had spent a little more time in the placement of these buildings, the effect would have been stunning.

Structures can add depth to your garden; they can lead the eye into the scene you are creating. In this chapter, rather than discussing building structures, I'll emphasize using them as part of your landscaping and creating a vignette or a town.

Just like plants, structures can be used as landscaping. Structures can give scale to your work and can accent certain features. A small Japanese maple (see page 94) can get lost in a large garden setting. However, if you place a miniature building alongside it, the maple is now accented. Structures can also add color to the garden, just as flowers do in a full-size garden landscape.

When designing your garden railroad, it's wise to consider providing open spaces to create the illusion of distance between towns. The illusion you will create is that of the time and distance to be traveled by the train. It is tempting to place structures everywhere there is space. On my railroad, I have certain areas designated as "no-build" zones.

If you are depicting a modern era railroad, all you have to do is look around the full-size world to see how structures are arranged. For earlier eras, you can study old photographs. In some cases, buildings were in straight rows. Often, buildings ran alongside the railroad tracks. In some cases, like during the Gold Rush era, the train's tracks ran down the middle of the street. Sometimes towns were built along a river or a stream bank. Some small towns were built around a town square or a central park, or homes had to be built on hillsides. As you can see, there are many ways to lay out a town.

The village of Fog Harbor developed around the railroad, just as many full-size towns did. Fog Harbor is a coastal town on my railroad. The operator is standing in the "ocean." The main line runs in front of the lighthouse/train station and behind the commercial row part of town. Spur tracks and sidings weave among the various structures. While structures on the main street are in a row, other structures are aligned perpendicular to the main street. This gives the town more depth.

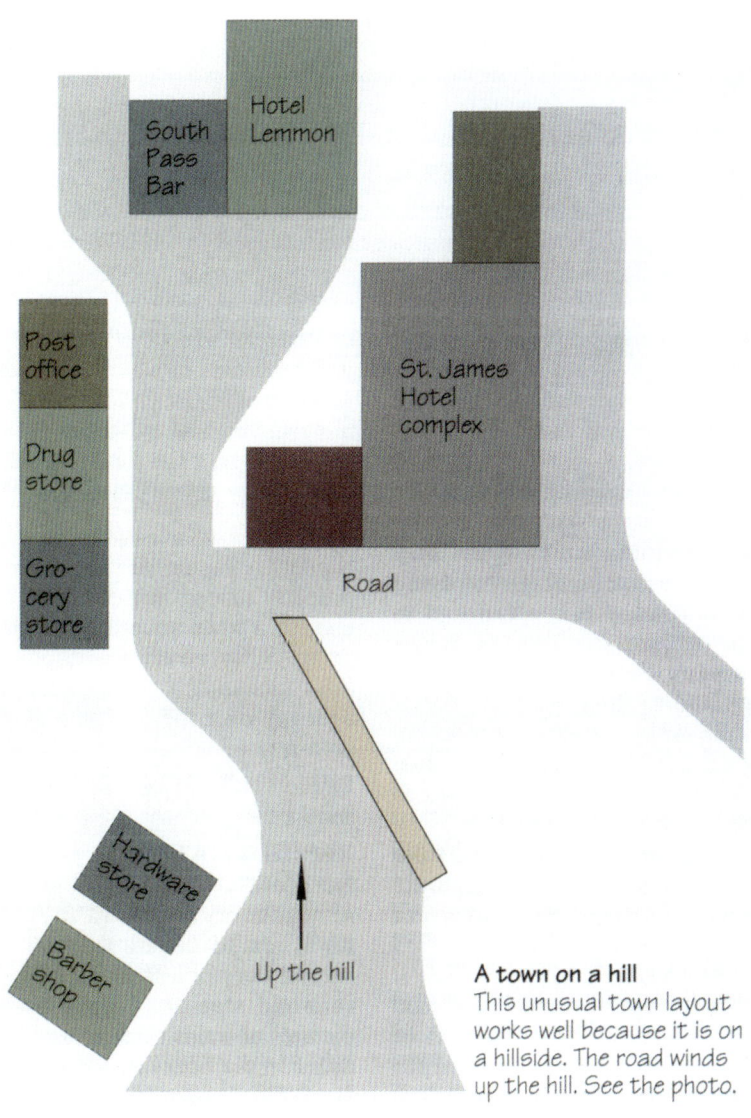

A town on a hill
This unusual town layout works well because it is on a hillside. The road winds up the hill. See the photo.

In Pacific Mills, a roadway with a parallel retaining wall allowed including more features in the given area. The buildings are raised higher than the railroad. This is a common practice that you see in everyday life. The road in this picture was made by cutting concrete paving stones to the needed width. Rebar was laid down the length of the future road. Mortar was spread over the rebar, then the paving stones were set in place and the seams were filled. When completed, the road was smooth but not quite smooth enough, so I applied a thin coat of underlayment cement. That coating was made smooth with a metal trowel. (I say smooth but when view closely there is a little bit of roughness that simulates a paved street.)

Planting structures

Here are a few guidelines I follow in setting my model structures into my railroad.

Don't overwhelm the space. Almost anything can be reproduced in scale except space. When a structure is placed into a space, it will often dominate the area. I have a pond that looks like a mountain lake (see below). In photos where there are no scale references, the lake looked large. I decided to add a small dock and a boat house. As soon as I set them in place, my lake appeared to shrink. The boat house gave scale to the scene and revealed that the pond was really not very big.

To offset this phenomenon, model smaller structures or work in a slightly smaller scale than the trains. I model my structures in 1:24 scale, but my trains are 1:20.3 scale. If I modeled structures in 1:20.3, I would not have room for them in my railroad, or I would have a lot fewer structures. As long they are not displayed too close to the trains, your structures will look natural.

Don't mix scales in close proximity of each other. For example, if I have a 1:24 structure, I would not display 1:20.3 scale (on the larger size) or 1:32 scale (on the smaller size) details next to the structure. This would draw attention to the scale difference.

Use caution in mixing scale figures. Placing a 1:20.3 scale person next to a 1:24 scale door would really draw attention to the scale difference. One fix for this problem is to make your doors 1:20.3 scale, even though the rest of the building is 1:24. In studying old photos, I noticed that some doors were very tall, so a large door may not be out of character.

Always level your structures to the ground. There are few things more annoying then seeing structures that are not level. Even in a real-life ghost town, when a structure that is leaning over and ready to collapse, it is usually still level at the base. To keep structures level, I like to install a base. We'll look at structure bases in detail later in this chapter.

Use low-growing ground covers around structures. Irish and Scotch moss, creeping mint, and green carpet sedum are good choices. Always select plants with small leaves for use around structures. Most plants have leaves that are larger than true scale, so be selective about the plants you use. Avoid flowering ground covers around structures (or remove the flowers), as the flowers are usually out of scale.

Miniature trees and shrubs make a scene come to life. Plant trees far enough away from your buildings to allow space for the tree to grow. Some trees can be pruned to avoid this problem. Other trees other grow too fast—avoid these. The same is true of ground covers. Aggressive plants, such as blue star creeper, will engulf a building in one growing season. Slower-growing plants like elfin thyme, Corsican mint, and Irish and Scotch moss are easier to control.

A consideration in placing structures in your landscaping is the creation of scale references. Without references to any common objects, this lake (left) could seem to be almost any size. Introducing the boat house created a size reference, so now we view the scene relative to the size and shape of a known object like a building. In most cases, the natural landscape will look smaller with structures in place (right).

Space permitting, a road and walkway should be added to the scene. With the exception of wilderness cabins, most buildings will have road access. You can add a road even if it does not connect to anything. The idea is to suggest a connection to other structures or places. Roads also provide detailing opportunities. You can display model cars and trucks or horse-drawn vehicles nearby.

Bases

Placing your buildings on bases serves several purposes. A base provides a solid platform upon which a structure can be set. You can level the base using a bulls-eye or a two-plane level. When the structure is placed on a level base, it will stand perfectly upright, adding realism by establishing balance.

A base also keeps a building out of the dirt, which is especially important for wood structures. Bases minimize mud splash down. If you have buildings outside, you know what I mean—you find mud splash all over them after a rain. (Placing mulch over exposed dirt reduces mud splatter as well.)

Bases also act as foundations. Extending a horizontal surface of a base can be used as a station platform, patio, boardwalk, or other similar surface.

I have experimented with a variety of materials and methods for making bases. Select a material that will not rot or warp. Concrete or cement products, such as pre-cast stepping stones and mortar, are good choices. Since I illuminate my structures, I pre-drill a hole in the base and pull the wires up through the hole, leaving a little extra wire sticking up.

Using stepping stones or pavers is fairly easy. Use a wet saw to cut the paver(s) to size. Dig out the area where the foundation is going to be placed, and add sand or soil to level the paver. Place your building on this pad.

Another way to make a base is to use Dura Rock, a cement product that looks like sheet rock. (See the photos below.) You can use a drywall knife or a saber saw to easily cut out a compli-

Woodside Community Church: A single miniature rose in a full-size garden may go completely unnoticed. When placed next to a miniature building, the rose becomes an accent that is now part of a larger scene and is more noticeable. The structure becomes a backdrop for the rose.

With Dura Rock, you can cut out a base just the way you want it, including walkways. The above photo shows several foundations cut and ready to be installed.

At right, the Dura Rock bases have been laid out. Notice the lighting wires have been pulled up through a hole cut into one base. The bases have been cemented in place. Mortar was placed on the ground and the Dura Rock pressed into the wet mortar. The bases were leveled and the excess mortar removed with a trowel.

A great little maple (Acer palm 'Tama Hime') is planted next to the California Furniture Store. These items compliment each other. The maple is more visible because it is next to a structure, and the scene is softened and given life by the presence of the maple tree. In the background, Herniaria Glabra Green Carpet is used.

Plants can add much to a scene, even to an industrial area like the Pacific Mill ore dump.

cated shape. Cut out the building's base first. Dig out the area approximately 2" deep where the base will be installed. Mix a batch of mortar or concrete and fill the hole with mortar mix. Take the cut-out Dura Rock sheet and push it into the wet mortar mix. Level the base and clean up the edges with a trowel. Let the mortar cure.

PVC foam board also makes a good base. Use a 1"-thick piece. Cut the PVC with woodworking tools. You can also scribe details into the surface to simulate expansion joints or decorative patterns.

Roads and streets

Roads and streets add dimension to a scene, and you can display autos, trucks, or other vehicles. A roadway becomes more interesting when curved. Curves tend to pull the eye into the scene, and make the roads look longer. Sometimes you might not have a logical place to end a road. In this case, you can use a theatrical trick called forced perspective. Gradually taper the road until it is out of the scene. You can also curve the roadway behind a sight block, such as a building or large rock.

Terrain

If you have terrain in your garden railroad, take advantage of it. In the full-size world, it is rare to find a completely flat spot, and it's not uncommon to see structures stepped into a gentle hillside or built on stilts. In some parts of my hometown, the street side of a house may be one story, and the back side three or four stories. In river country, houses were often built on pilings. These types of foundations will give your town and buildings an extra dimension.

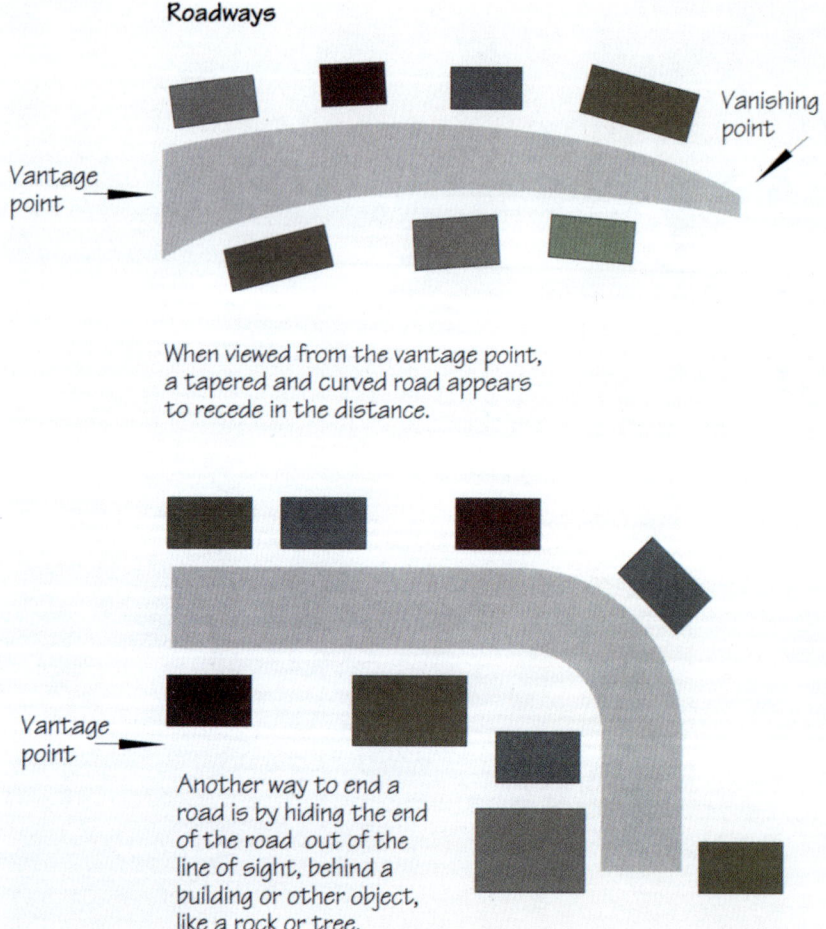

Road Building

In this series of photos, I am building a permanent road. First, I excavated the area. Since this is a long roadway, I installed rebar to prevent cracking in the event that the ground settles. I used concrete mix to make the sub-roadbed, and leveled the track on this concrete base. For a road without track, this would be one of the final steps. The concrete would be toweled out smooth.

Since the tracks will be imbedded in the road, I used mortar as a finish topping. Mortar does not have gravel in it, so it is possible to spread this over the track. I spread the mortar completely over the track, and troweled the roadway smooth. Using an old railroad car truck, I cut flangeways into the wet mortar by running the truck over the mortar. After 24 hours, I ran the trucks over the track again and removed any excess mortar that I might have missed the first time. You can still easily scrape mortar at this state, since it is not fully cured. You may need to repeat this process several times to clear the flangeways and remove mortar from the rail heads. Finally, polish the rail heads with an abrasive track-cleaning pad.

The most permanent way to create a road is by pouring concrete. Be sure your road is in its final location, since re-doing this process is not an easy task. Make your road from concrete mix. Mix it according to the instructions on the bag. Make a form or just trowel it by hand. Use a steel trowel to smooth out the surface. If you are not happy with the finish, try using thin set or self-leveling cement to get a smoother finish. I use concrete stain, available in home-supply centers, to color my roads. Black stain looks like an oiled or asphalt road; brown or tan can simulate a dirt road. For a gravel road, glue down model-railroad ballast using concrete adhesive.

Cap stones, cast cement pieces used to cap off block walls, also make nice roadways. First, dig out the roadway and pour mortar mix in the hole. Push the cap stones into the wet cement. To prevent cracking in between the stones, I lay a piece of re-bar in the wet cement under the cap stones. Level the cap stones and fill in the spaces between the blocks. Aside from the grooves, you have a pre-made smooth surface. This method works especially well as a base to apply thin-set cement to create a smooth surface, or as a base for a gravel road, where you would glue model railroad ballast.

Use Precision Board as a base for your roadways. This material works just like Styrofoam, but it is far more durable. You can texture it to look like stone, brick, blocks or concrete.

A less permanent way to make a road is to use "¼" fines" materials. Sometimes called gold dust, decomposed granite, blue fines, quarry fines, or quarry waste, this is crushed rock in ¼" or smaller sizes with a lot of dust in it. This material packs down hard when watered in, and can be made even harder by adding Portland cement.

To add cement, dry-mix 4 or 5 parts ¼" fines to 1 part Portland cement. Spread this mixture out dry, then lightly spray it with water to set it. I like to spread the material with a trowel to form roads, then mist it with a garden hose. Dirt roads can be simulated with Gold Dust, which—as the name implies—is yellow or gold in color.

Here is the nearly finished product. Homes in the background have been installed, and two buildings in the foreground have been placed on their bases. Notice on the left end there is an empty lot. This is where another building is placed for open house days. This building is stored indoors, but with a foundation in place, it can easily be installed as needed.

Wall lamps in this cozy social establishment not only light up the room but also highlight the fixtures themselves. These were made with miniature light bulbs and miniature beads.

CHAPTER

15

Lighting

As a young boy, I was fascinated by an illuminated sign my Uncle John owned, which showed the San Francisco Oakland Bay Bridge with the San Francisco skyline in the background. The scene changed from day to night every two minutes. In night mode, all you could see were dimly lit windows and a soft glowing background (simulating sunset) silhouetting the structures. Unfortunately, we cannot bring the sun up at will on our outdoor railways, but we can control what we see at night.

The great thing about the dark of night is that you can create a unique scene. You can light just the things you want to see, and everything else will be out of sight. (Just think of the mistakes you can hide!) My lights are on a timer. I enjoy seeing the dimly lit windows and porches as well as the small twinkling street lights.

Lighting is quite simple to install. You can buy an outdoor lighting transformer such as you would get with a set of Malibu lights. I don't use the included lights, since they are too large. Instead, I use miniature lamps, such as the ones sold by Miniatronics and Micro-Mark. I use 14-volt lamps that draw 50mA. You can run them a long time on a 12-volt transformer. A 50mA rating means you can run up to 20 of these on one amp at 12 volts. (The lights that come with a Malibu light kit draw 1 amp each.)

Lighting effects

There are three types of lighting for garden railways.

1. Light emitted from within a structure, such as through a window or door opening.
2. Light sources outside of the structure, such as from porch lights, work lights, or street lamps.
3. Natural light, such as moonlight.

Lighting structures

A soft glow coming through a structure's windows is more desirable than seeing a bright light bulb shining inside the center of the structure. The 50mA lamps, for instance, are not as bright as the lights supplied with the Malibu light kit, so there is no need to diffuse them. Since they use far less power, you can use multiple bulbs if needed.

A quick and easy way to mount a lamp is to mount the light bulb in a tube, such as a piece of K&S brass tubing or Evergreen plastic tubing. Run the wires down the tube to the main power line. The conduit holds the lamp up in position so the light sticks up out of the ground (like a candle). Set the structure down over the light. Your building is still easily removed or taken indoors, as no wires are connected to it.

Mount the light high enough so you can't see the bulb itself, or use window coverings such as curtains or shades to disguise the bulb. Fog or frost the windows to diffuse the light. See the chapter on making windows.

Nine-volt battery clips make good inexpensive plugs. You will need two. One is connected to the mainline 12-volt power, and the other is connected to the building's lights.

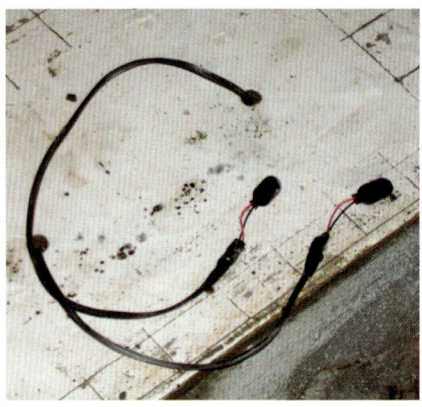

To connect to the main power source, drill a hole through the base through which the hook-up wire is fed.

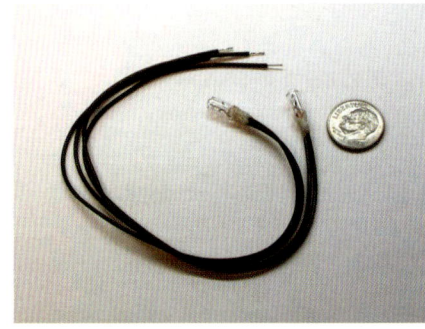

Lamps like these 14-volt 50mA examples are ideal for use as building lights. They last for a long time when run on 12 volts. The bulb is molded onto the end of the wires so there is no need for a light socket.

If needed, make a reflector from aluminum-colored duct tape. Apply the tape to the inside of the roof, reflecting the light downward.

You can also mount lights to interior walls above the window openings. Use

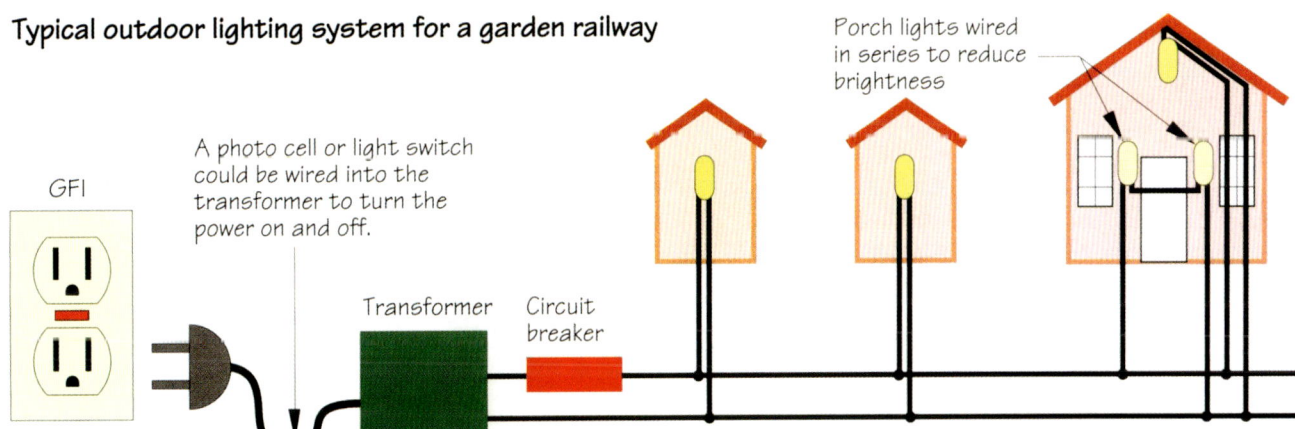

Typical outdoor lighting system for a garden railway

NOTE: The main line from the transformer should be 12 or 14 gauge direct-burial cable. Individual lines for buildings can be as small as 20 gauge. The insulation on these wires should be neoprene or other weatherproof material.

Making a desk lamp

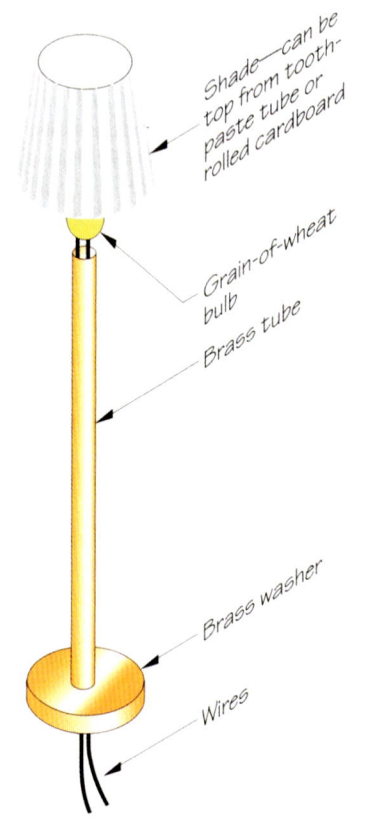

Pole or floor lamp

Desk lamp: I made the light on the piano from a wooden bead for a base, a piece of costume jewelry, and acrylic. Craft shops are sources of odds-and-ends to make lamps.

This industrial-type kitchen lamp is made from a Plastruct lamp shade. The dispenser end of an empty tube of glue could make a similar shade.

silicone to hold them in place. I wire the lights together, and connect them to a 9-volt battery clip. Then I install a second battery clip on the mainline wire, allowing me to connect and disconnect the buildings easily as needed. I've used this method for several years with no rust or corrosion problems.

Protective grease is good idea in areas with harsh soil conditions. If your building has a full interior, use copper tape (sold at miniatures or dollhouse stores) for wiring. It's designed to be hidden under wallpaper or to be painted over.

Sometimes interior lights shine through walls, so the entire building appears to glow. Rectify the problem with a coat of dark paint on the interior walls.

Another method of lighting is to simulate desk lamps, table lights, or street lamps. In this case you would make a lamp using a grain-of-wheat (GOW) light. Even a 12-volt GOW bulb puts a lot of light, so it may need to be dimmed to create the desired effect. Making two lamps and wiring them in series will dim them.

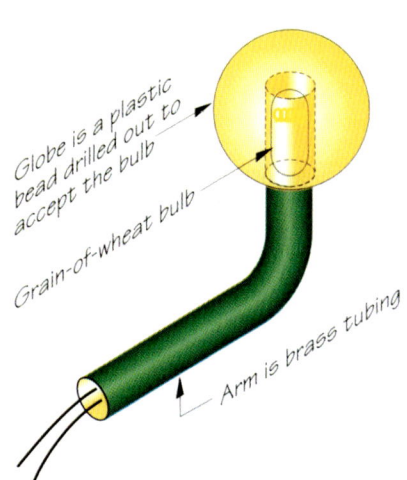
Porch light

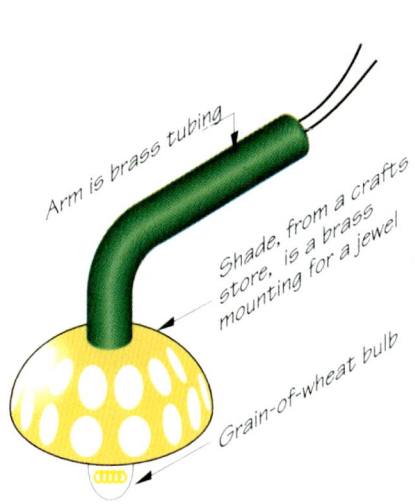
Fancy porch light

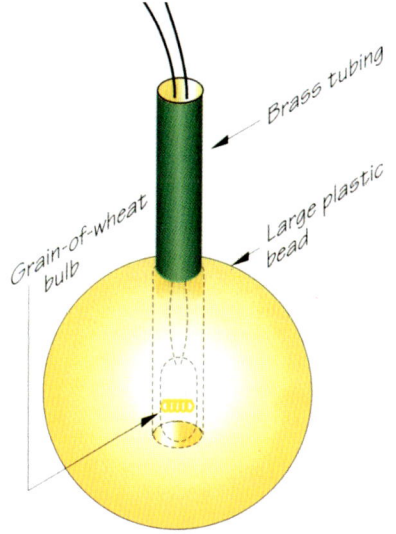
Hanging porch light

Another source of light that comes from a building comes from porch lights or, in the case of industries, area lights (right). Porch lights almost always look better when wired in series. Area lights, however, can be brighter. See page 100 for information on series and parallel circuits.

Making light fixtures

Create an area light for an industry from the top of a glue tube. Cut off the top part of the tube and feed the wires from a GOW bulb through the neck from the tube side. Once the bulb is snug against the inside of the tube, add a piece of piano wire or brass rod (about 1/32") to the wire bundle. Place a piece of heat-shrink tubing over the wires and the neck and bend the wire to the desired shape. Heat the shrink tubing to tighten it around the newly created shaft.

Make porch lights from plastic beads. Drill out the hole in the bead large enough to accept a GOW bulb. Make a bracket from a piece of brass tubing. Insert the wire into the tube and bend the tube to the desired shape to form the bracket.

Miniature garden lights can be made using GOW bulbs and brass tubing. See the drawing at right. Cut a ½"-long piece of 1/8" brass tubing and insert a GOW bulb. Use the tubing alone or add a bracket by soldering a piece of brass wire to the tube. Paint it black.

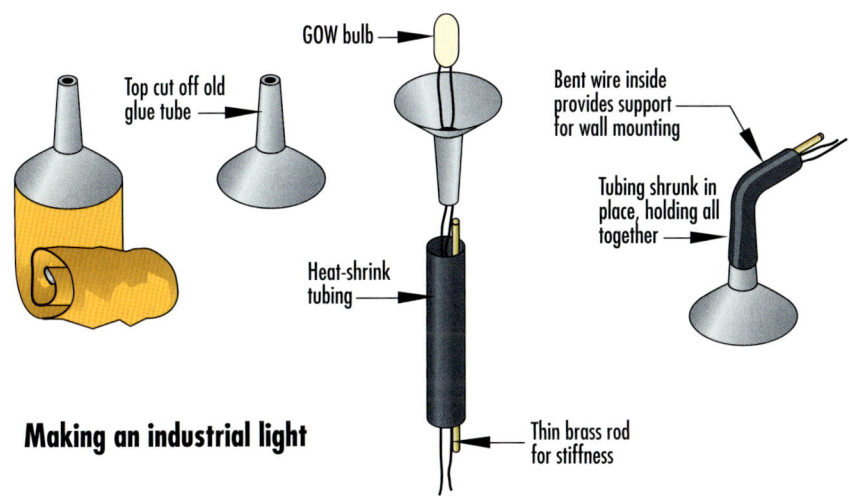

Making an industrial light

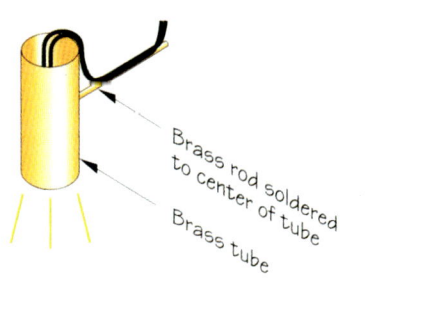

This fixture can be stuck in the ground and used as up lighting for trees and the walls of buildings.

Miniature garden lights

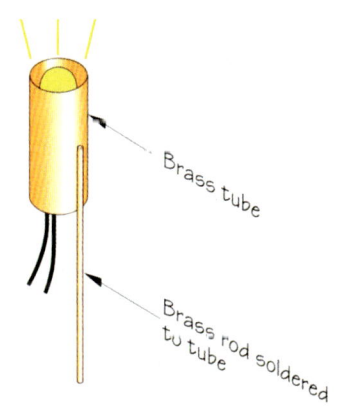

This fixture can be mounted in trees and used as down lights to wash the trunks and the ground below.

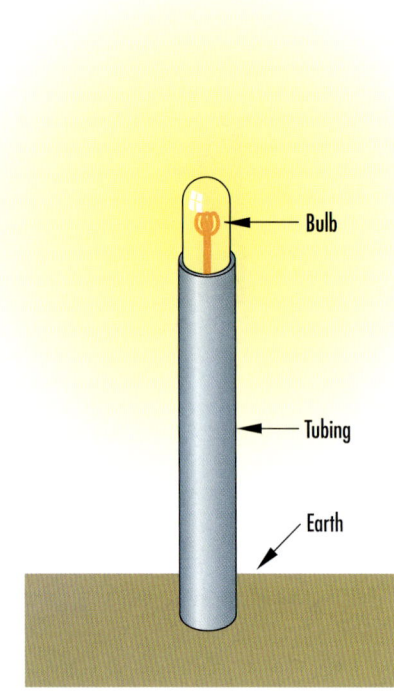

Light mounted on a piece of tubing

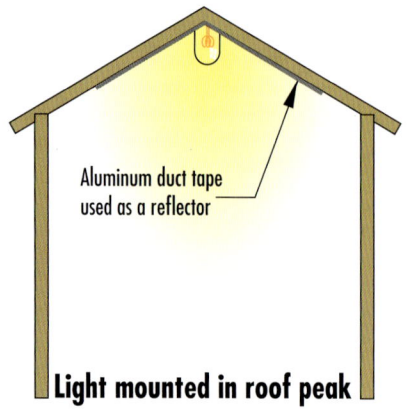

Light mounted in roof peak

Craft shops carry odd-and-ends to make a perfect desk lamp. Make a simple lamp from a plastic bead and a plastic hood or toothpaste cap for a shade. Run the wire through the hole in the bead (sometimes the hole must be drilled larger). Glue the shade to the GOW bulb with silicone or CA glue.

Creating moonlight

Moonlight shines on the top of your structures. You really don't want a shine, but more of a glow. Create moonlight by using one or more low-intensity lights. Mount these lights in trees or on fences. The key to making this look authentic is to hide the source of light. You want to see the effect of the light, but not the light itself. As the light shines through the foliage, it's filtered and softened, making it less noticeable. You may need to use several lights overlapping in coverage to get this effect over a large area.

Other full-size garden features can be highlighted by garden lights. A tree, for example, can be lit up like lightning by placing a light at is base and aiming it up into the branches.

You can buy a low-voltage submersible light to put in your pond. This will also look like moonlight if set up right.

The lighting system

The best system for outdoor lighting is a 12-volt system. A low-voltage system like this is safe, is not hazardous to humans or pets, and can be buried without conduit.

The heart of the low voltage system is the step-down transformer. The step-down transformer reduces your 110-volt household power down to a safer low voltage. Transformers are available in a variety of voltages, but for garden lights, 12 volts is the industry standard. Low-voltage lights run on AC or DC current.

The amount of amperage or wattage required is dependant on how many lights you want to run. See Watt's Law for power below. A simple way to calculate your wattage is to estimate the number of lights you are going to use, add up their total wattage, then factor in 10 percent to 20 percent more for safety. It doesn't hurt anything to have a transformer with a higher capacity (that is amperage, not voltage). The reserve power may come in handy if you decide to expand the railroad.

Hardware stores and home improvement stores carry transformers designed for outdoor garden lights. Some even come with built-in timers and are enclosed in a protective case. You can use an ordinary transformer if you take care to mount it in a dry area, such as inside one of your buildings. If the transformer is not equipped with one, install a circuit breaker on the output side equal to its capacity. The primary side, or high voltage side, should be connected to a GFI receptacle.

As a beginner, it is often cheaper to buy an outdoor lighting kit, which

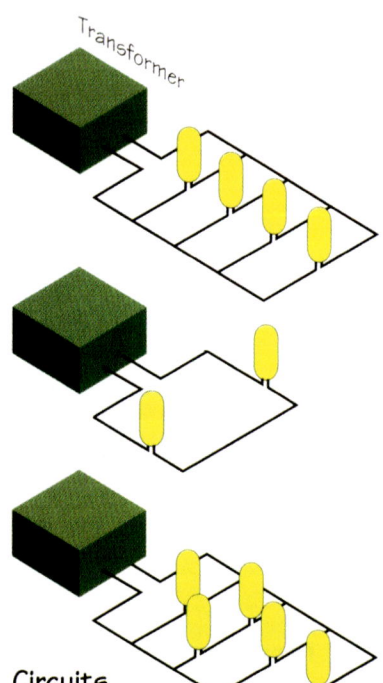

Circuits

Parallel circuit. Each light receives the same voltage, but the amperage is divided. Our miniature lights should always be wired in parallel except for special effects.

Series circuit. In this circuit, the voltage is divided between the two lights. Since each lamp receives only half the voltage, each will be dimmer than normal.

Combination circuit. The two bulbs in the second row from the transformer are wired in series, while the rest are wired in parallel. This circuit is useful for times when you need dimmer lights within a larger circuit—a pair of porch lights, for instance.

includes a transformer, direct burial cable, and lights. Check the transformer's output power to make sure you'll have enough power to run all your lights. Usually, these kits come with a dozen light fixtures, which is about the maximum the supplied transformer can handle. You can run more lights if you use smaller 14-volt hobby lights, like a GOW bulbs. These burn less energy and provide a good low-intensity source of light.

I was surprised to learn that some small 12-volt automotive lights burn as much as 1 amp (or more). Miniature hobby lights, in comparison, use about 50 milliamps (mA). (There are 1,000 mA in 1 amp.) You can run 20 miniature lamps with the same amount of energy it would take to run one automotive lamp.

Powering your structures can be done in a couple of ways. If you plan carefully, you can run conduit to each future building site and pull the wire through as needed.

I prefer a simpler, more flexible method. Since we are using 12 volts, we can use direct burial cable, easily available at hardware stores. This cable is designed to be used outside and can be run over the surface or underground. It is UV stabilized and is relatively tough, although a pick or shovel could cut it if you accidentally struck it. At 12 volts, though, there is no danger of electric shock if you damage the cable.

Using direct burial cable makes it easier to retro-fit lighting since you do not have to dig a trench and bury conduit. You can run the line on the surface, or bury it just below the surface. Run the cable to each town or group of structures. Once the line is there, branch off of it as needed.

Generally, lights are wired in parallel (see page 100). This way each light gets the same voltage, and if one goes out, the others in the circuit do not go out.

Series wiring cuts the voltage down by the number of added lights. For example, if you connect two 12 volts lights in series, each gets 6 volts. This is useful when you wish to cut down the brightness. Lights in series generally last longer because they are not burning at full intensity. In general, though, do not wire lights in series.

Hanging lamp and pull string: This is an old-fashioned hanging light bulb with a pull string. It is simple but believable. This type of light could also be found in logging shacks and other lesser-type structures.

Splicing

Hardware stores and home centers sell underground splice casing, a tube containing an insulating grease. The splice is inserted into the tube. I prefer to solder the splices and wrap them in insulating tape instead.

A solderless insulation-piercing splice is also available. It works by placing two wires into the splice connector, then compressing them. I suggest not using these for garden lighting.

WATT'S LAW FOR POWER IS:

$P = I \times E$

$I = P / E$

$E = P / I$

P is power in VA (volt amps) or watts

I is current (intensity) in amps

E is voltage (electromotive force) in volts

Gallery

Detailing the Crystal Club Bar

This building is one of only two structures on my railroad that do not stay outside. The main reason is the interior detailing. Spiders and bugs love to get inside model structures and make webs and a general mess.

My wife, Pauline, and I have been working on our Crystal Springs Railroad & Lumber Co. since 1988. Each town on the CSR&L has a saloon or two, so when it was time to remodel the town of Maple Estates, I decided to start with the corner bar, and thought it would be fun to create a full interior. I had good working knowledge of what goes on in a tavern, having spent a summer working in my uncle's restaurant-and-bar establishment.

My Crystal Club would have a main room with bar and back bar, tables and chairs, and such accessories as a pinball machine, piano, and jukebox. Food from the kitchen would arrive via a pass-through window. The back alley would have a garbage can and old boxes. Alongside would be a newsstand, complete with magazines and newspapers appropriate for its the era, circa 1939.

I enjoyed making this model, but the most fun comes from watching people looking at it, especially when they touch the piano keys and hear the piano play.

Follow along with the photos and captions as I describe my Crystal Club and the source of many of its details.

The bar building
My Crystal Club bar was built to 1/24 scale and was designed to be removed from the layout and stored indoors. It is mounted on a base of cement board that was coated with Fixall so I could carve in sidewalk seams and cracks with a hobby knife. The sidewalk extends out from the bar on two sides, since this is a corner establishment.

Walls
The walls were built up from sheets of cast resin "bricks." Using my own molds, I cast two types of brick sheets—one with deep mortar lines for the exterior and the other with more shallow mortar lines and a smoother appearance for the interior. (Chapter 11 explains how.) Openings were cut in the walls to fit Grandt Line cast windows and doors.

Paint and mortar
The exterior walls were spray-painted with Ruddy Brown primer, then coated with Builder's Choice latex paint (BC21 Brick Red). After the paint dried, I "picked out" individual bricks with several acrylic colors including Tuscan Red, Cranberry, Dark Red, and Black. When this was dry, I used Andi Mini Brick & Stone Mortar (AM0239B Dark Gray) to fill in the

mortar lines. I applied it with my fingers and rubbed it into the cracks.

Curtains and awnings
The curtains and awnings were made from paper. I made a color photocopy of real fabric and reduced it to 1:24 scale. Then I ran off a sheet and worked it into shape. Even on close inspection you cannot tell it is paper.

Barroom Interior
The interior brick walls were painted white. The floor and wainscoting in the barroom were made from hardwood veneer. The bar and back bar were made from mahogany purchased at a dollhouse store.

The figures
My patrons were a lucky find—two of my favorite characters—Stan Laurel and Oliver Hardy. They are standing at the bar.

The pictures
I made pictures for the walls by scanning and reducing images from several books and magazines with on my scanner/printer. To indicate the bar's pedigree and age, certain pictures were selected. My Crystal Club is set in the late 1930s, so a 1939 calendar hangs on a wall in the bar, and there is another in the kitchen. A picture of Franklin D. Roosevelt, taken in 1936, hangs on another wall. The proprietor's son is serving in the U.S. Navy, and a photo of his ship hangs on the wall above the pinball machine. Several patrons of the bar work in the lumber business, and they donated a picture of a lumber schooner. A representative collection of saloon art hangs on the other walls.

Tables and chairs
The tables and chairs were made from wood turnings from a craft store. The chair legs and backs are brass wire, bent to shape.

Money
I reduced a dollar bill to 1/24 scale on my scanner, then printed multiple copies for the currency that's sitting on the bar. The coins are simply small pieces of copper and aluminum cut out and hammered flat.

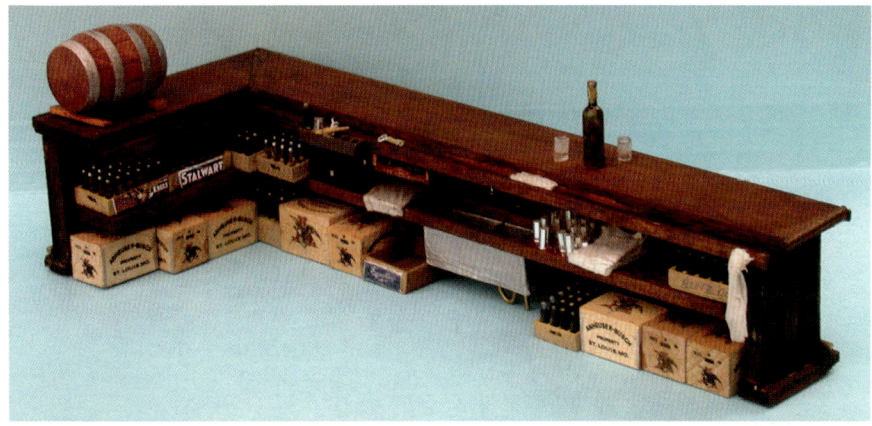

Jukebox
The jukebox started out as a plastic refrigerator magnet. First I made a mold from this magnet. But before pouring the casting, I made a row of "records" and a record player/changer. When I poured the clear casting resin into my mold, I embedded the records and player in the uncured resin—along with a 14-volt bulb. When the casting cured, I could look through the window in the jukebox and see the records and player. Translucent glass paint was then applied to sections of the jukebox that should be lit up, and opaque paint covers parts where light should not show through.

Toy train
The train on the shelf is a dollhouse miniature, and represents a cast iron toy train.

Piano
The piano is one of those details that makes my barroom seem complete. It is a refrigerator magnet with a small battery and electronic chip. It actually plays two bars of music from *The Entertainer*. The original refrigerator magnet was too shiny, so I dulled it by spraying it with flat finish. I then added flowers, sheet music, an ashtray, and a working lamp.

Glasses
The beer and shot glasses were made from acrylic tubing. For stemware, straight pins formed the base and stem, and a bead represents the glass itself.

Mirrors
The mirrors were cut from an acrylic mirror sheet. The traditional "first dollar" hangs on the back bar's mirror.

Bottles
The bottles on the back bar are cast resin. First I turned a master bottle on my lathe. Then I made a mold from it and cast enough bottles in clear resin for the row. Next I modified some of them by doing such things as squaring their sides or shortening them. Once I had a half-dozen different shapes, I put several of each shape together and made molds that allowed me to cast dozens of bottles at a time. Blue/green, yellow, and brown bottles were produced by adding a little pigment to the clear resin. Most of the labels are reductions of actual liquor bottle labels reduced to 1:24 scale on my scanner/printer. A few were drawn and reduced.

Behind the bar
A small shelf behind the bar holds a 1/24 scale revolver. The bottle opener was made from thin wire twisted to

Gallery

form an eye and worked into shape. The corkscrew is a styrene shaving glued to a small wooden handle.

Boxes
The Budweiser (Anheuser-Busch) beer cases are taken from a 1/24 scale beer truck. The other boxes were cast in resin, and their labels were made in the same way as the labels of the bottles on the back bar.

Spittoons
I turned the spittoons from brass. In studying photos of old saloons, I noticed that the aim of many patrons was not so good. It looked like there was as much on the floor as there was in the spittoons, so I could not resist adding this detail.

Ashtrays
Cutting the bottoms off cast resin bottles and drilling out the resulting piece made ashtrays. Cigarettes and butts were made from wire painted white, and their ashes are represented by a little thinned black paint.

Pretzels
The pretzels were formed from thin wire and painted. The bowl is Magic Sculpt.

Pinball Machine
I made the pinball machine's cabinet from mahogany—the legs are wood angles. A photo of a real backboard was reduced to scale. I fashioned the "playing field" from translucent white acrylic, with "pins" made of painted pin-heads. The guides, flippers, and coin slot are all styrene. Both the backboard and playing field are covered with clear styrene and backlit with 14-volt bulbs.

Newsstand
I have been collecting 1/12 scale dollhouse vintage newspapers, post cards, magazines, and books for many years. I reduced some of them to 1/24 scale for use in the Crystal Club's newsstand. There are reproductions of the covers of Hollywood movie magazines and news magazines such as *Life*. I even reduced some dollhouse newspapers and added headlines appropriate for 1939. For example, one headline reads, "Nazis invade Poland."

Kitchen
The stove is a refrigerator magnet. I scratchbuilt a master refrigerator and cast it in resin, adding claw feet from one of my cast resin bathtubs. The sink is also cast resin—it has a complete piping including a hole down the drain. The bar of soap is a piece of styrene, while cups and saucers are dollhouse parts. Food prepared in the compact kitchen is passed to the bar through a kitchen service window.

Washroom
The dollhouse toilet has a scratchbuilt seat with a flush box and chain. There is a resin sink, plumber's helper on the floor, and a scratchbuilt roll of toilet paper. A bare light bulb illuminates the room.

Back alley
The door on the left opens into the kitchen and is guarded by a yellow bar cat—the door on the right opens into the washroom. Notice the gumball machine in front of the newsstand and the bundle of newly delivered papers.

Animating a steam-operated sawmill

When I decided to build a new mill, I wanted visitors to see the inside. I wanted it to have an animated "working" log haul, carriage, main husk, edger, and cut-off saw. In studying local logging history, I learned that most of the sawmills once located on the San Francisco Peninsula were open sided, with a roof and not much more—perfect for my model.

My mill is not a model of any particular sawmill, but a composite of features from sawmills I like. One that particularly impressed me was the Frase Creek Steam Sawmill. I saw it in a video—this small sawmill in the state of Washington was still operating in the late 1980s. Its owner had salvaged steam engines from ships, mills and other industries to power it, giving it that homemade/make-do look I wanted in my model. The Frase Creek mill looked as though it had been built in the Depression era, and had salvaged many parts for its own "homemade" equipment.

The mill building

A 1:24 scale sawmill is large. Since I have no room indoors to store a

Gallery

SOURCES

Air Motors (now sold as E-Z Air Pneumatic Motion Control Actuators)
California & Oregon Coast Railway
P.O. Box 57, Rogue River, OR 97537, 800/866-8635, www.cocry.com.

Drive components such as belts, chain, pulleys, bearings, gears, couplings, mounts and hardware. (The author used 6M-712 Plastic Sub-Miniature Roller Chain and matching chain sprockets):
Stock Drive Products/ Sterling Instruments
2101 Jericho Turnpike, P.O. Box 5416, New Hyde Park, NY 11042, 516/328-3300. Fax 516/326-8827, www.sdp-si.com.

No. 10V & No. 10H steam engines:
Cole Power Models, Inc.
5539 Riverton Ave., North Hollywood, CA 91601, 818/762-0272.

Operating Ice Loader kit with Tamiya "ladder-chain and sprocket set" (#70142), and brass dogs:
M-Tech
4005 Seaport Blvd., West Sacramento, CA 95691, 916/373-9974

building this size, my model had to be weather resistant from the start. It also had to be accessible for maintenance right on the site where it was installed. The wood pieces were glued with Titebond III waterproof wood glue. Wherever possible, wood parts were also nailed using an 18-gauge brad gun.

The framework and flooring are redwood. I added extra vertical posts to the frame to make the structure sturdy enough to be tilted on its side, letting me reach under the floor to access the carriage drive motor and cable there.

A saw filer's shop occupies a loft above the main cutting floor. On the prototype, a small traveling block-and-tackle was used to hoist saw blades up through an opening in the floor. Saws from the logging operations would also be worked on in the saw filer's shop.

I sheathed the roof with corrugated metal formed by pressing aluminum flashing into a die. The corrugated panels were glued to the sub-roof with GE Silicone II.

At first I thought I could just build the sawmill and simulate the "working" machines inside with dummies made of blocks of wood and a saw blade or two. I found that it is difficult to pull this off in large scale because everything is so big. So I decided I needed machines that "worked." Since there are no commercially available large scale machines for sawmills, I had to scratchbuild them all—giving me a mill that looks like its machines were "homemade."

Since space was limited in my sawmill, I decided to make a rough-cut mill designed to cut logs into planks or into square timbers. To do this, I needed a husk to cut slabs from the logs, an edger to cut the planks to a certain width, and a cut-off saw to cut the planks to desired lengths. I figured that it would not be difficult to animate these machines.

I used Western Scale Models' kits and Bill Gustafson's book *The Sierra Railroad Machine Shop*, so I already knew how a line shaft works. I was able to apply that information to my mill.

The mill machines

The Log Haul lifts logs up out of the pond to the log deck. I bought an M-Tech Operating Ice Loader kit. This kit has a Tamiya "ladder-chain and sprocket set" (No. 70142), and a number of brass dogs made by M-Tech that fit on the ladder chain, which were ideal for my sawmill. However, my log haul is so long that I had to buy two extra chain kits and some extra dogs. I mounted a 60:1 gear head motor run the chain. My log haul can actually move logs.

The log deck is animated by air from under the deck provided by air motors (actuators) like those used to control turnouts on a model railroad. These work like a hydraulic cylinder and have a spring return. The air provided jiggles the log so that it appears to be hung up. The mill worker seems to be trying to free it.

The husk has a maple wood frame. I made a mandrel from a brass rod to accept a Makita 4-inch-diameter saw blade. I set this mandrel in ball bearings in the wood frame. A drive sprocket was then friction fitted onto the mandrel. This saw will actually cut wood, but there is no safe way to hold the wood in place so I don't demonstrate this feature.

The carriage runs back and forth on two rails laid on the floor of the sawmill. The 12-volt motor that powers the carriage has a 16:1 gear head and a pulley mounted on its shaft. The motor is mounted below the floor of the sawmill at the center of the track. I cut an access hole in the floor so I could see this mechanism, and have access to the drive for maintenance.

At each end of the track is a screen door roller like those used on a sliding screen door, mounted on the center line, halfway above and below the floor. A "rope" connected to the left end of the carriage runs around the left roller, wraps around the pulley at the center of the track once, and runs to the right hand roller. After it runs around the right roller once it is tied to the right end of the carriage. I used a double slipknot at each end of the carriage so I can tighten the rope as necessary. As the pulley rotates, it pulls one end of the cable in and lets the other end out, moving the carriage back and forth.

The edger was the most interesting machine to make. An edger has several parallel saw blades and a pair of live rolls that rotate in the opposite direction of the saw blades. These rolls pull the lumber into the machine. The saw blades are set at various distances apart to cut boards to the desired widths.

I made my edger using five Gyro brand, 1"-diameter circular saw blades mounted on a brass shaft in a superstructure made from styrene. The blades were installed on a drive shaft using

Gallery

CA (cyanoacrylate adhesive) to hold them in place. This shaft is also used to power the rollers. Since the rollers must rotate in the opposite direction from the saw blades, the drive chain is run on top of the drive pulley giving reverse rotation. While the saw blades and live rolls are animated, the rest of the machine is static.

The cut-off saw has a wood frame hanging on a line shaft. The saw is powered from the line shaft. A figure, the "sawyer," runs the saw. Air from my compressor powers an air motor located in the rafters. This air pushes the saw frame back and forth. The sawyer has a movable arm attached to the wood frame so it looks like he is moving the saw across the board to be cut. The line shaft passes through a pair of ball bearing at the top of the frame. The line shaft turns, but the weight of the saw frame keeps it from spinning around. since the saw does oscillate, a counterweight made from a bucket filled with scrap metal pulls the saw away from the operator when he lets go, and keeps the saw from oscillating while it is idle.

Line shafts and steam engines: Two line shafts transfer power from two steam engines to the husk, edger, and cut-off saw. All the shafts have ball bearings mounted in special laser-cut hangers to reduce friction. Ladder chain sprockets were installed on the line shafts. At each machine, a large sprocket on the line shaft, and a smaller one on the machine produce a gear ratio of about 2:1.

I wanted to have two different steam engines to drive my line shafts. The engines are from Cole Model Power, a company that specializes in miniature power plants, such as live steam engines and small internal combustion engines. They run like a top. Lubrication is supplied by an in-line oilier. I used a No. 10 H, a horizontal steam engine, to power the husk and the edger. My second engine, a No. 10 V, is a vertical steam engine that runs the cut-off saw. These engines can be run on live steam or air. Since live steam means having to tend a boiler, I chose to run them on compressed air. I do have a small boiler that can be used for show, and have run a steam line from this boiler to the exhaust stack on my sawmill. This lets me pipe steam into the stack. The exhaust air from the engines causes the steam to rise in puffs.

I find that my animated sawmill really adds a lot to my layout. It is always popular during an open house. I am looking forward to building an animated live steam stamp mill as my next challenge.

REFERENCES

Frase Creek Steam Sawmill, Selective Eye Video Prod., P.O. Box 1521, Chehalis, WA 98532.

Gustafson, Bill. The Sierra Railroad Machine Shop, Western Scale Models, 19441 Business Center Dr. #107, Northridge, CA 91234, 818/341-7862 fax 818/341-7864, www.westernscalemodels.com.

Shaffer, Reg. "The Saw Mill Chronicles," Narrow Gauge and Shortline Gazette, July/August 1984 through January/February 1986 (all are out of print).

Detailing Brown's Machine Shop

Brown's Machine Shop in place on the author's Crystal Springs Railroad & Lumber Co. Operator Aaron Theisen on the left is running a steam locomotive with that radio controller. Photo, courtesy of Large Scale On-Line (www.largescaleonline.com).

For Brown's Machine shop, my main reference was Bill Gustafson's *The Sierra Railroad Machine Shop*. It houses 1:20.3 machines that are produced by Bill's company—Western Scale Models. Since lathes and such come in many sizes, I thought these fine 1:20.3 machines were close enough to use in my 1:24 building. (Western Scale Models also produces these machines in ¼" scale.)

I began the machine shop by creating a floor plan. After building a foundation and adding floor joists and sills, I installed individual floorboards. The walls were framed prototypically with redwood beams cut from ordinary fence boards pre-stained with alcohol and India ink. Waterproof glues (Titebond II, Ambroid, and Silicone) hold the beams, joists, and floorboards in place. Although I plan to store this building indoors, these glues make the machine shop weather-resistant enough that if I have to, I can leave it outdoors for a few days.

For the corrugated siding, I formed heavy-duty aluminum foil in a die and painted it with gray primer from a spray can. As I glued this siding in place and weathered it with chalks, the metal got bent in places making the building look like it has had some heavy use.

Brown's Machine Shop has a removable roof so visitors can view the interior details. However, the roof trusses had to be installed as part of the building because they hold brackets for the line shafts that drive the machines. With the roof trusses part of the structure itself, I needed a way to make a roof that would hold its shape when removed. Looking around, I came across a large piece of galvanized sheet metal. Cut to shape, bent to fit, and covered with sheets of my corrugated metal siding, this sheet metal was perfect.

The corrugated metal siding is held in place with Silicone, and the roof can be easily lifted off the trusses. Many of the machine shop's details were put in place before I installed the Western Scale Models machines. I wanted to include things that you would see in a real machine shop. The photos show the result of my efforts—small tools, cans, and accessories line the walls, and lean, sit, or hang from the beams. "Swarf" from the lathes and other debris clutters the floor. With the roof trusses already in place, installing these details was kind of like building a ship in a bottle.

The interior details include tools from Bachmann and Ozark Miniatures, and parts from model vehicle kits I had in my scrap box. The "open" cans were cut from aluminum tubing; the closed cans are short pieces of wood dowel. Their labels are color copies I made at my local copy shop using my collection of reproductions of old can labels and

Gallery

The overhead line shaft with its pulley wheels, belts, and brackets was difficult to install. The machines are 1:20.3 scale kits from Western Scale Models.

Note the calendar, clock, and thermometer on the vertical beams. The litter on the floor shows that this machine shop is a working industry.

The entire machine shop with the roof removed reveals its many details.

advertising. I find items for this collection in books, old magazines, and even in dollhouse stores. The calendar and "metal" wall thermometer are also color copies.

When I made the color copies, I reduced them to the proper scale. The can labels were cut out and glued on the cans. The calendar was hung, and before placing the thermometer, I added a little piece of acrylic rod to simulate the glass tube that held mercury. The clock is a button I found in a local craft shop.

Finally, the Western Scale Models machines were assembled, painted, and installed. The line shaft parts were painted gray, and any "running" surfaces —such as pulley wheel faces—were polished. The belts that drive the machines were made from thin cardboard painted brown. Installing the belts and line shafts in this nearly completed building was tricky. I kept wanting to reach in through the walls. However, Bill's book was an excellent guide, and helped me understand exactly how a line shaft works. Once the machines, shafts, and belts were in place, I added working lights: 14-volt grain-of-wheat bulbs mounted in home-cast resin reflectors.

I am very pleased with my Brown's Machine Shop. It provides an interesting industry for my Crystal Springs Railroad—even though I do have to take it in at night.

Dedication

To my partner in the railroad, in the garden, and in my life—my wife, Pauline.

Acknowledgments

About three years ago as president of the Bay Area Garden Railway Society (BAGRS), I started a group formed mostly of club members interested in model building and researching better ways to build models for outdoors. We have shared information and experience about building materials, glues and adhesives, building techniques, and many other subjects concerning outdoor structures. I want to acknowledge their help and thank them for their many contributions to the hobby.

BAGRS Advance Modeling Group
    Bob Brown
    Dave Connery
    Bruce Jahn
    Dart & Dot Rinefort
    Eric Maschwitz
    Henner Meinhold
    Russ Miller
    Kermit Paul
    Ken Martin (a contributor though not an official member)

I also want to extend a special acknowledgement and thank you to
    TAP Plastics
    3011 Alvarado Street
    San Leandro, CA 94577

… and to store manager Russ Miller (yes, the same Russ Miller as above), for the company's support and assistance in compiling the technical information on plastics and on glues and adhesives.

About the author

Jack Verducci has always had an interest in models and miniatures. He built his first layout (HO scale) with his brother as a Boy Scout project and discovered large-scale trains during his time in the Navy. In 1988, he built the initial version of his Crystal Springs Railroad, and a few years later, Jack began building garden railroads professionally. Since that time, he has built nearly 75 garden railroads in many areas of the country. He has earned the National Model Railroad Association's (NMRA) title of Master Model Railroader based on his garden-railroad accomplishments. Jack is a regular contributor to *Garden Railways* magazine. His Garden Railway Design & Construction column has appeared regularly in the magazine since December 1996. Jack lives in the San Francisco Bay area.

We cover Garden railroading from every angle

More great books to help you with your garden railroad!

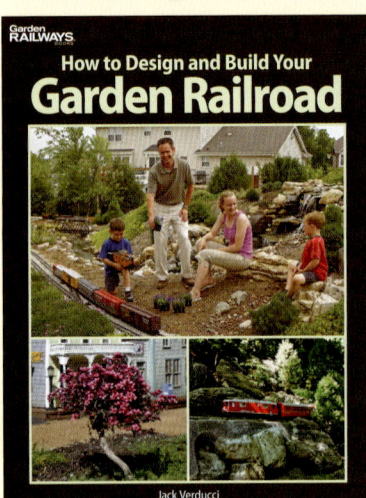

Increase your knowledge and skills with tips for designing, planning, and installing a layout; landscaping with natural materials; adding drama with structures, bridges, and trestles; and designing and installing water features – all shown in beautiful full color.
12406 • $21.95

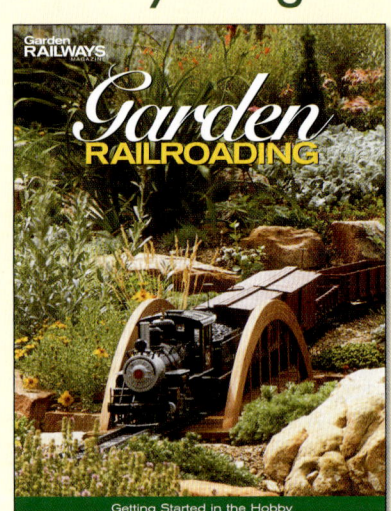

This comprehensive collection of informative articles from *Garden Railways* magazine addresses the main topics of the hobby such as site considerations, developing a plan, landscaping, trackwork, power, and gardening.
12217 • $22.95

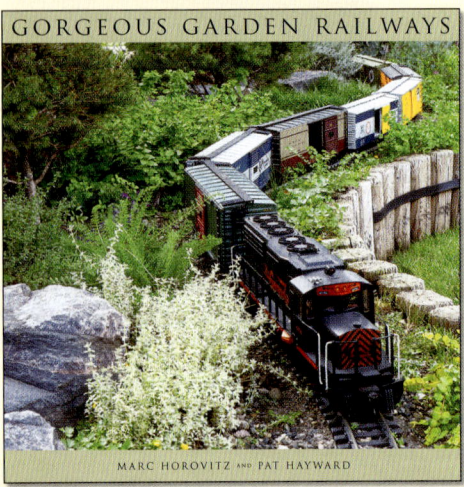

Enjoy vivid photography and informative text as you learn more about garden railroad landscaping, trains, infrastructure, ponds and water features, and other landscape challenges.
62326 • $24.95

Model railroaders with green thumbs will learn the basics of garden railroading with this handy booklet full of tips on everything from choosing plants to arranging the track to best suit the terrain of your yard.
12415 • $7.95

Buy now from hobby shops! To find a store near you, visit www.HobbyRetailer.com

www.KalmbachStore.com or call 1-800-533-6644

Monday – Friday, 8:30 a.m. – 4:30 p.m. CST. Outside the United States and Canada call 262-796-8776, ext. 661.